The Magic of Writing

Also by Adrian May

Myth and Creative Writing (Longmans, 2011; Routledge, 2014).

Songs and Poems:
An Essex Attitude (Wivenbooks, 2009).
Ballads of Bohemian Essex (Wivenbooks, 2011).
Comedy of Masculinity (with CD album: Wivenbooks, 2014).
Discovering England (with CD album: Wivenbooks, 2017).

Adrian May

The Magic of Writing

First published 2018 by
PALGRAVE

Palgrave in the UK is an imprint of Macmillan Publishers Limited, registered in England, company number 785998, of 4 Crinan Street, London, N1 9XW.

Palgrave® and Macmillan® are registered trademarks in the United States, the United Kingdom, Europe and other countries.

ISBN 978–1–137–60800–0 hardback
ISBN 978–1–137–60797–3 paperback

This book is printed on paper suitable for recycling and made from fully managed and sustained forest sources. Logging, pulping and manufacturing processes are expected to conform to the environmental regulations of the country of origin.

A catalogue record for this book is available from the British Library.

A catalog record for this book is available from the Library of Congress.

To all the students of my Writing Magic MA class at the University of Essex, past, present and future. To all the writers, friends and colleagues who helped and encouraged me, particularly Kate Powis, for conversations and reading.

Acknowledgement

Thanks to Hilary Llewellyn-Williams and Seren Books for: Hilary Llewellyn-Williams: 'Hazel/Coll' from 'The Tree Calendar', in *Hummadruz* (Seren, 1987).

Contents

Preface

Who is *The Magic of Writing* for?

All writers feel that there is some magic about good writing, which they hope to achieve themselves, or at least to approach. All students and teachers of creative writing at the adult level, and all serious writers, can benefit from taking this idea intelligently and practically, thereby getting the magic of writing working for them. Magic connects strongly to creativity, is of interest as a subject, and as a purpose of good writing, which always seeks to uncover hidden truths and meanings.

When poet Dylan Thomas published his collected poems in 1952, the verses are prefaced with a note that offers a kind of ritual dedicatory blessing, which he sees as necessary, even as it is given with an ironic turn of phrase. Reminding ourselves of the serious mysteries of how we make and express art can be fruitful for writer and reader alike. Definitions of the term 'magic' are discussed in Chapter 1, in terms of its usefulness to writers.

The book is written in an accessible, essayistic style, as the purpose is to communicate and pass on useful ideas and exercises to writers and teachers. It is intended to be an inspiring book, and one about inspiration. *The Magic of Writing* is dedicated, in Dylan Thomas necessary way, to all my own students and my fellow writers, known and unknown.

What is the Book Saying?

The Magic of Writing as a title suggests that writing has a magical element to its creation, its messages and purposes and often in its underlying concerns. In chapters on the magic of words themselves and about the idea of 'portals', for example, readers will begin to see the act of writing in this light.

Chapters on meeting magicians and on tricksters not only can add depth to character creation, but can offer the subject of magic as itself significant. Chapters on key writers Yeats and Shakespeare, and their huge influences from magic, offer models of depth and composition, while the big subjects of animals, love, endings of all kinds and the future offer a deep way into the mysteries of life, via magical perspectives. Magical subjects like the Tarot and the Muses offer patterns of creation and thought which writers have found continually helpful.

While the book is in no way aimed at writers of fantasy, it certainly does not exclude people interested in that genre, but its scope is more towards all creative writing students or literary writers. Again, while not specifically for those who want to step towards 'magic realism' and the innovations of a Borges, for instance, the book seeks to expand the imaginative scope of all writers.

No book on such a wide and hard-to-define subject area can hope to be comprehensive, but this one covers some areas which feel immediately useful to writing, from a writer's perspective, and seeks to send you on your own journeys of discovery and research.

How Does the Book Work?

Each chapter contains an essay on an aspect or use of magic and its relation to writing, and discussions of texts related to the topic, with examples of writers directly or indirectly using the elements from it. Related writing exercises are included, as are creative examples from the author, specially written for the book.

The Magic of Writing can be used as the basis for a class or writing group's sessions, or by a reader/writer seeking to deepen and sharpen their practice, through discussion, reading and writing. Direct quotations from contemporary sources are kept to a minimum, as permissions are often difficult to obtain. Readers may want to use the internet to read some materials referred to, where they are often easily found.

I hope that the positive energy found in the writing of the book will work its connective spell on you, and inspire you in all your writing.

Introduction: Magic and Literature

Literary Magic

Marina Warner, author of *Signs and Wonders* (2003), is one of the best writers and scholars on all the strange tales of the world. When I asked her about the idea for this book, her answer was unequivocal. The history of literature, she told me, is inextricably tied up with magic and magical ideas. My tentative thoughts were immediately put into focus. If you think of *Oedipus, The Tempest, Faust, A Christmas Carol, Silas Marner*, and of writers like W.B. Yeats, Borges and Angela Carter, magic is at the centre of these works and authors. The more I began to see magic as central to writing, the more I found it everywhere in literature. Like myth, magic is the hidden element, in its many guises, of human creativity and in its journeys of discovery and self-discovery.

Writers have always had this sense of approaching what is hidden, what is occult, and have naturally tuned into these kinds of thoughts. Even writers of the most minimal of 'dirty realism' do not neglect the mysteries of human life. Take one of Raymond Carver's barest stories, often used to demonstrate his plain style, 'I Could See the Smallest Things' (*What We Talk About When We Talk About Love*, 1981). The story is about a woman awake at night beside her sleeping husband. She gets up and walks outside and has a brief conversation with a neighbour. The story takes place at night and the strange quality of the moonlight illuminates the title. An alternative, mysterious clarity ensues, acknowledged in an ironic remark about seeing a face in the moon. The otherness of the whole experience is like a revelation of realities that are hidden in the glare of daylight, however minimally written the tale seems. Moonlight here is not romantic but a different kind of reality, or epiphany, a kind of clear night of the soul. Arguably the spare quality of the writing highlights, in the strange clarity of moonlight, the mystery, rather than diminishing it.

Being able to see this aspect of the literary is beginning to read as a writer, who seeks depth in a shallow world. Magic is a big subject, the whole of it beyond our scope, but aspects of it show direct usefulness to writers and the book seeks to explore some of those most accessible. The chapters of this book cover magic in relation to words, another direct link to all writing; to persons and characters who have magical elements to them; to key writers who use magic in their methods and works; systems of thought and divination; supernatural beings; animals; and we end with the magic of love, endings and the future. Including the mythic power of narrative and symbol, magical ideas can be seen as portals of creative power.

Human life is partly occult. We have an inner life which only reveals itself partially, sometimes hidden even from ourselves. Literature, like myth and psychology, is concerned with it. Writers, in themselves and in their subjects, are only too aware of this. Magic therefore works in the way that mythic or metaphorical literary writing does, in seeking to reveal hidden connections and truths.

Writers have always used the trickery of fictional invention, the hidden meanings of symbol, myth and psychology, to achieve depth, both in their writing and in its process of invention. The direct connection of myth to magic is then in the symbolic and in the supernatural. The natural and psychological processes myths suggest can also link myth to magic. Literary writing and myth are connected to magic again by their approach to the mysterious elements of creativity. Like myth and creativity, magic has change as a central concern.

If we look at the use of the magical element in J.B. Priestley's play *An Inspector Calls* (1945), we can see again that magic can be used for clarity and to serve realism rather than to add mystery or obscurity. Priestley was influenced by J.W. Dunne's *An Experiment with Time*, with its reflections on precognition. The revelation that the titular Inspector does not actually seem to exist, but seemed to know all the visited family's dark secrets, offers an overview of moral clarity, as if from a bird's-eye view, and all human vanity seems exposed to the light.

The history of magic, both as a subject for writing, with its colourful characters and events, and in its use of ritual and archetype as well as its themes of transformation, offers many possibilities for writing. The practice of magic also has much in common with the creative process. The message writing seeks to convey is often one which renews the vision and seeks a revelation away from limited ways of seeing the world. Great writers are magicians in several senses and they tackle the mysteries of power, of love, of death, of life itself.

The more we seem ruled by science, by computerised mathematics linked to selling to us in a more controlled way, the more we cling to what cannot be measured but which seems to make life worth living. The ritual of reading makes us summon up invisible lives, persons and truths. We breathe another's air and give shape to invisible forms. Dream to dream, the writer sings the reader, who joins in.

Magic is 'Magic'

Magic is everywhere, even, or especially, when denied. Our rational surfaces are constantly challenged by irrationality and we seek outlets for it in the madness of love, the wildness of nature or dissipation, in our dreams and flights of fancy. We feel lucky, or unlucky; we feel connections to some people; and we are drawn towards the mysteries of otherness. The idea, first identified as such by Sir James Frazer in his book *The Golden Bough* (published between 1890 and 1915), is called 'sympathetic magic', where 'like' can affect 'like' and the world of the imagination is thus directly linked to the world of things. The link of mind and matter must be at the centre of literary work, as it mimics the thing it seeks to affect. In a sense, divination, ceremony and ritual and symbolic patterns of meaning all take part in this kind of magic, where the world is full of meaning and influences.

This book does not require you instantly to believe in a sensationalist spread of obvious supernaturalisms, but an open mind will help. There is a sense in which we cannot help believing in magic. If someone tells you that a garment was once worn by a murderer, would you wear it yourself? Our minds make the magic and 'gut feelings' are trusted and tested every day. We might not all go to the fortune teller but we often feel on the brink of knowing more than we can prove and we invest our lives with meaning with the connective thoughts and fancies which make us more alive.

When I began writing this book, I had a sense that I should write a chapter about the Muses before anything else, as a kind of evocation of the spirit of the tradition of magic and writing. On the Monday I started, BBC Radio 4's long-running series *In Our Time* featured a programme on the Muses. I was completely unaware of this being broadcast on that same day, but the coincidence has a synchronous effect on my confidence.

This kind of thing is not unusual with writers, where connections become more available to the openly creative imagination. At the same time as my Muse coincidence, I read of Don DeLillo talking about the flow of sentences being a kind of magical occurrence This is active and sympathetic magic at work in normal life and especially in writing. Magic is recognising the power and potential of the mind, even at the most basic level. People talk of good days, good 'vibes', great atmospheres. We might call it part of religion, or psychology, or art, but our lives are created in our own sense of aliveness through such vitalising examples.

The 'magical thinking' of childhood is often used as an example of innocent foolishness, but writers are often, and usefully, told to think as a child. The clarity of vision writers seek is a place where words are brought to vivid life and everyone knows that the spontaneity of response and impulse of the creative is connected to a kind of open potentially of experiments in just that kind of innocence.

Magic that seeks to know the future, or oracular divination, is a kind of concentration on the present moment, seeking hints of meaning and connective patterns to the future. If time has meaning, then these methods can become useful. Finding them useful proves they work, reflecting and focusing the mind. Literary prophecy tells the hidden truth of now and of what follows. Again, magic acknowledges that meaning is everywhere.

The colloquial use of the word 'magic' as a term of general approval might be useful as it is, if it means positive, connected up and enabling your life, and writing, to feel meaningful.

Writing is Magic

If you are a serious writer, you already accept that life has meaning beyond mere rationality – otherwise you would be studying science. Creativity as a kind of process is a withdrawal from the world in order to recreate it in a more meaningful way and has the quality of a ritual – a shaman-istic self-induced crisis of remaking. It is easy to forget how strange an activity writing actually is, if looked at this way. W.H. Auden's favourite story of Henry James is 'The Private Life' (1892), where a writer is seen simultaneously at work in a dark room of a hotel, while socialising in a bar downstairs. To Auden, this illustrates the mystery of literary creativ-ity. The spookiness of writing must not be overlooked.

For creative writers, magical ideas can provide an antidote to the ten-dency towards the formulaic. It is perhaps in the interests of critics, experts, publishers and teachers to downplay the mysteries of writing. I have recently read about W.B. Yeats' interest in the occult (see Chapter 12), which he insisted was central to everything he wrote, dismissed by a critic as a kind of hobby. Likewise a biographer of Bob Dylan, who holds a similarly magical view of songwriting, dismisses this interest in magic as meaningless nonsense. These commentators are not men capable themselves of writing anything of the quality of those whose thoughts they dismiss. Yet this kind of fearful put-down is all too common and amounts to what critic Harold Bloom called the work of the 'School of Resentment' (*The Western Canon*, 1994).

Writers are practical magicians and make no apologies for embracing what helps them achieve their creative ends, sometimes to the embar-rassment of the business that depends on them. Everyone is aware of the dull competence that can be achieved in the 'workshop' and even with the 'tools' rather than 'rules' versions of the predominant creative writing cultures, as they are taught. The kind of 'fame school' courses offered do nothing to help this as they are bound by commercial con-straints and imply that a sense of career entitlement can make you a writer. What they illustrate rather is that would-be writers are suggest-ible to the unspoken feeling that being near a famous tutor/writer will infect them magically. Magic can call to vanity as well as to clarity, but it can highlight both.

The practicalities of writing using magical influences can help writers towards inspiration in direct ways and remind them that writing must involve the width of their imagination where other approaches may, however unintentionally, impose limits. Magic offers a tradition of ways into what is hidden, where the real strength of both creativity and the lit-erary work itself can be found.

Some magical ideas help return us to a sense of the aliveness of the world, like those of natural, animistic, synchronous or sympathetic versions of a kind of nature worship. But magic can also look towards a new super-awareness of the future and the edge of new 'science'. It is the oldest and newest form of renewal.

Magic can obviously offer negatives as well as positives, as far as writing is concerned. I always ask my own students to give me examples of both in our initial discussions for our classes. Direct use of magic, they have suggested, in content especially can be lazy, unbelievable, trivial, silly, lost in fantasy, easy to dismiss, out of control, nuts, childish, clichéd, escapist, overlooked, an easy excuse, baffling or dodging reality. Sensible writers avoid this, after the ritual naming of these demons.

On the other hand, they have variously offered positives: atmosphere, transformations, new directions, a breaking of boundaries, a sense of wonder, 'what-if' possibilities, access to what is hidden, the exploration of the irrational, an embracing of what is unexpected, secret knowledge, symbolic depth, the timeless, the taboo (forbidden and special), changes in consciousness, an opening up of potentialities, and access to rites of passage and mythic patterns and rituals. Magic is parallel to art, as Shakespeare suggested in *The Tempest*, and can lead to folly as well as to wisdom, but there seems no denying 'the alchemy of the word'. This phrase is the title of a section of Rimbaud's poem 'A Season in Hell'.

Elements of magic used in writing echo the creative process. The Inspector in *An Inspector Calls* is like the absent presence of the creative artist's bird's-eye view, seeing all that is hidden. When Wordsworth writes 'The world is too much with us' (Sonnet 33, 1807), we know he means the world of 'getting and spending' and therefore offers an alternative world view, which is wider and sees through surfaces, as a writer must do. This is creative magic.

There is something active and practical about ideas of magic which match the performative elements of writing and communicating. In the chapters that follow, via concepts and subjects, methods and myths, we will seek a natural magic of grounded thoughts and exercises that show the connections between magic and writing and the possibilities offered to those who would give life to their creative work. And it is not all solemn. There is comedy in magic too – for example, that available via the negative aspects of its direct use, as listed above.

Used as a subject, a way of thinking creatively and of revealing the need to address and acknowledge the mysteries and varieties of human life and experience, magic, used overtly or as an underlying influence, can put just that, the magic, into your writing.

Write About

Everyone knows a spooky story, or perhaps an urban myth, of some kind. Tell us yours.

Describe an artist taken over by a strange, new creativity.

Has something strange happened to you when writing, like an experience of 'flow', or coincidence?

Create a dialogue between a sceptical and positive view of creative magic.

Magical Texts and Literary Examples

Books about magic are many and varied and all can offer something useful for a writer, as research or raw material. I buy them both discriminately and indiscriminately, following my nose and interests. I usually ask my students to read Colin Wilson's *The Occult* and Lindsay Clarke's novel as a way of introducing the scope and application of the subject to a writer. A few other reliably useful texts are listed below.

Some Background and Indicative Reading

Lindsay Clarke. *The Chymical Wedding* (1989).
Intelligent literary fiction with magical themes.

David Conway. *Magic: An Occult Primer* (1988).
Practical ways to use real magic.

Owen Davies. *Magic: A Very Short Introduction* (2012).
Excellent for history and academic context.

John Fowles. *The Magus* (1966; 1977).
A very good novel about magic and rites of passage.

Rosemary Ellen Guiley. *Harper's Encyclopaedia of Mystical and Paranormal Experience* (1991).
A sensible dictionary-type book, of which there are many.

Christopher Partridge (ed.). *The Occult World* (2015).
Recent and fascinating academic survey of whole subject area.

Colin Wilson. *The Occult* (1971).
Still the best and most positive, creative overview of the subject.

1

Magic is a Dirty Word

Magic, like writing, can never be quite respectable. How does a successful writer do it? Are they trying to be cleverer than you? Who do they think they are? Surely anyone can write. People can feel that something suspect is going on or that someone is tricking us while, at the same time, gaining some advantage over us.

The search for some way into the secrets of the irrational involves the mind and the creative self being open to possibilities the conventional might justly shun. Magic, like writing, is always on the brink of breaking down the order which we tend to make, and to feel safe within. Thinking differently, finding a difficult or hidden insight, can be dangerous or a threat to the bland order of things. Attempts to make magic or writing respectable are doomed to failure.

A writer needs to use this subversive energy, which is from the same source, so that writing itself can offer the surprise of a new clarity of vision, a fresh idea or a revealed pattern to see under the surface of things. A writer is a Fool, as in Shakespeare, who takes licence to tell the strangest truth.

Writing workshops, creative writing degrees and even books like this often seem to deny the dark, often secret nature of the creative, but even in these places, space must be given to the mysterious and peculiar nature of creative quality. Even if we start with a scholarly look at the definition of the word, a rational and consistent picture may not emerge. We teeter on the brink of nonsense, of incoherence, of trickery and charlatanism, as much as shamanism.

The *Oxford English Dictionary*'s definition begins in an unpromisingly promising way for our purposes, by saying magic is 'the pretended art'.

This immediately makes me think of my response when creative writing students show fear of being pretentious. I suggest they answer their doubting selves in an assertive way by saying: *you* are pretentious; *I* am creative.

There are two sides to magic indicated here also. One is 'influencing events by compelling the agency of spiritual beings' and the other is 'bringing into operation some occult controlling principal of nature'. Like myth and religion, the supernatural side of magic is always there, but also the psychological or even scientific discovery of natural patterns and cycles. The occult means what is hidden from us. Magic, like writing, seeks to see what we normally are blind to. If people think we are dangerous or pretentious, it shows us that we are on to something.

A writer's definition of magic might be: *A way of accepting that what is beyond us and may seem impossible is worth our attention, as it is directly connected to creativity and potentially fruitful for creative work.*

It is obviously the supernatural element of magic that might be troubling to many. But if we think of the supernatural as symbolising this notion that there is always something beyond us, and that this is as it should be, we can at least see it as part of the wonder and mystery of life and death. The supernatural embodies the spirit of the multiplicity of creativity, as well as obvious narrative benefits.

There seems to be an etymological link with the word 'magister' in magic, where 'magister' means some kind of master. It is arguable that people go through two stages of maturation. The first is where they gain some kind of worldly knowledge and rationality, where the adult ego is acquisitive and strong; the second might be the second sight or mastery of letting go some of that ego to embrace the possibility of renewal and self-driven creativity. Writers on the occult call this 'twice-born'. Youth has a natural creativity, a natural mastery, but the loss of magic in the rational mind is familiar to us. The midlife crisis is a loss of worldly mastery. The writer loses early promise and seeks to regain it.

J.H. Retner described this problem in *The Diary of a Modern Alchemist* (1974). In chapter one, 'The Real Adventure', he says that for a while we are content with 'material comfort and success', but eventually 'every achievement merely creates the desire for more'. Later, 'we begin to perceive that the only real adventure is that of life itself'. We lose knowledge and seek wisdom.

Can this wisdom be restored by trickery, by stumbling into the world of fakery and the wacky? The 'mind, body, spirit' section, 'MBS', is surely just 'miscellaneous bullshit', as my friend Lance Rickman says. But we sense also there is something beyond us, something wider and potentially more profound than the world of narrow materialism.

This second maturation might also be the reason why excessively 'rational' people (and many politicians) seem absurd to us. Somehow they have made a fetish of their religion of rational and material progress. To the mind of, possibly, the older or wiser ordinary person, not averse to notions of deeper truth, it is, paradoxically, the politicians who begin to look like fakes. Have you ever noticed how politicians overuse the word 'clear'? These are the real fakes who point to the magician or writer and call them the 'mountebanks'. Authority distrusts a magic writer. Our insecurity seeks someone who is less authentic, or more authentic, but in a less obvious way.

Creative Example

The Fortune Seller

The writer must risk everything
Stumbling into the arena
Where the cheap trick is promised
And shown to be a sham
And yet the people come

And it is an act
But, as the fortune seller told you
When you pulled back her curtain
What is not an act?
Who has an exclusive on the real?

Not the muddy banker
Scrabbling in the ground for his count
When nothing seems to count
Or amount to much

But the fortune seller in the shabby booth on the pier
Who tells me how tired she is
As seeing the truth sought for in poor, rich souls
Wears her out with giving

Feeling wider, you think
You pay first because, first foolish
It becomes magic

This poem could also be written (or rewritten) as a story, where a sceptic visits a seaside-pier fortune teller. Anger and doubt in the customer give way to wonder, when genuine insight is shown. See also the 'Write About' section at the end of the chapter.

Eliphas Levi's classic study of magic was first published in 1860 as *Histoire de la Magique*, and the English translation by A.E. Waite in 1913. He begins by saying that 'Magic has been confounded too long with the jugglery of mountebanks, the hallucinations of disordered minds and the crimes of certain unusual malefactors.' His seriousness is emphasised at the end of the first paragraph of his introduction by his flat definition, saying that magic 'is the exact and absolute science of Nature and her laws'. There is no doubt that the great claims of magic as the source of much wisdom and subsequent thought, from the Magi to the roots of science in the alchemists, are valid to a huge degree. His book is an indispensable survey and useful to anyone with a real interest in the subject and its implications.

Magic, though, like all mythic material, has a tendency to hide its arts in the trivial and the vulgar and disreputable. For writers, that is part of its interest. The range of its reach, from the sternest scientist to the cheapest fantasist or cheat, is part of its trickster-like appeal. We demand seriousness and we demand doubt and we demand the carnival of masks, tricks and revelation.

Translator A.E. Waite was a member of the Golden Dawn, which included, at times, writers such as W.B. Yeats, also wished for magic to be serious. There is fun to be had with taking the serious seriously, and, of course, less than seriously. Levi was not averse to minor deception himself, as his real name was Alphonse Constant. He himself would make a good basis for a piece of fiction.

The interest in magic around the turn of the nineteenth century was echoed in the 1960s, when Richard Cavendish published his book *The Black Arts* (1967). Looking at his beginning, he says that 'black magic is the hunger for power', which he links with the Garden of Eden and the Promethean desire for men to 'be as Gods', as Genesis has it. In chapter one he also says that 'It is natural to think of magic as a thing of the past, which must have withered to dust under the hard light of modern science and scepticism, but in fact this is not the case. Magical thinking is still deeply embedded in human mentality.'

Cavendish's claim for magic as part of human thinking is an indication of the power of the human imagination and thus we can see the connection to writing, via our own version of creative or 'sympathetic magic'.

He also points out that 'No one is a black magician in his own eyes.' Here again we have the paradox of those who claim magic as their own. Like the witch-hunts and persecutions of history, any seeker after some insight can be seen as threatening orthodoxy and convention. My contention is that the writer-as-magician can accept this and use it in their known way and that creativity and magic share this strength, to challenge the surface of the world into a useful renewal of vision.

Twenty years later, Cavendish's *A History of Magic* (1987) emphasises the power of writing as magic. Writing was unavailable to most at its beginnings, but still maintains its power over us, from officialdom and bureaucracy to the potency of poetry. We can wield this magic for our own ends, as creative or literary writing has run like a shadow behind the writing of power or authority.

An example of a contemporary novelist whose work uses magical themes, albeit indirectly in literary novels, is Rupert Thompson. In *Divided Kingdom* (2005), Great Britain has been divided into sectors according to the old concept of humours, or personality types. His protagonist finds a nightclub, in Aquaville, which is in the Blue Quarter of the 'phlegmatic' or watery type of person, most prone to mutability and hence to magic. This is a place where the impossible becomes possible upon entry. Setting this place as a recreational, late-night event, he plays with the idea that magic and insight are not always located in a serious, or serious-seeming place. Thompson's novel is a great example of how an old magical idea can be used in a contemporary, literary novel.

The great Argentinean 'magic realist' writer Jorge Luis Borges' 'fiction' about the phoenix must have the last word on the subjectivity of magic. Magic needs its subjective power, we might say, in order to maintain something. Its elusive quality is a metaphor for its need for it to stay beyond us. Magic deals with making the unknown known, however briefly. However, it does necessarily rely on the unknown and the unknowable, which is only temporarily available to our narrow minds and feelings. Magic is concerned with what is outside our boundaries, what is inherently unstable and ignored by the many. This is where it connects to our creative insights, as we have seen.

In 'The Sect of the Phoenix', from the English translations of Borges' work collected in *Labyrinths* (1964), we hear about 'men of the Secret', which is 'sacred but always somewhat ridiculous; its performance is furtive and even clandestine and the adept do not speak of it'. The darker, truer element is elusive, with 'no decent words to name it, but it is understood that all words name it, or, rather, inevitably allude to it'.

He seems here, 'inevitably', to be talking of writing, of literature. The penultimate sentence of the 'fiction' reads, 'What is odd is that the Secret was not lost long ago; in spite of the vicissitudes of the universe, in spite of wars and exoduses, it reaches, awesomely, all the faithful.'

The mysteries of writing have also often been depicted as a kind of trick. Nabokov's *Pale Fire* (1962) is a classic of the clash between rational critic and creative writer, while Michael Frayn's *The Trick of It* (1989) charts a similar journey more directly. In the opening of the novel an academic has invited a female writer to lecture and he cannot quite believe she has agreed, after refusing several times. 'Now, of course, I can't help asking myself why? Why is she coming? What's in it for her?' The anxiety in the face of creativity is made manifest. Of course, the critic in these works stands for our own rational side, doubting something which came to us easily as an inspiration has any validity in the world. Creative duality is part of our strength. This is the ability to embrace the rational with wider possibility, as this is where our work resides.

The prophet is made to feel a fraud and, like Cassandra, cursed never to be believed. Ted Hughes' poem 'Famous Poet' illustrates this dilemma. This is someone who has hit something strong, but cannot repeat it. In the poem, the protagonist's early work 'Burst with such pyrotechnics the dull world gaped/And "Repeat that!" still they cry.' This poem, from *The Hawk in the Rain* (1957), was written very early in Hughes' writing life. The same collection contains his own famous poem of inspiration 'The Thought-Fox', marking his cleaving to his own creativity over the world's view of the 'monster' of the famous poet 'set/To blink behind bars at the zoo.' In 'Famous Poet', however, the protagonist is reduced to something 'wrecked' and obsolete, and he cannot 'concoct' what they want.

So writers and magicians must get used to the indignities of their craft and must face the suspicion of the world, who say, like poet Martin Newell suggests and others think, 'I could write like you I bet/Though, I've not quite started yet' (from 'Well Done, You!' in *The Wife of '55*. Nasty Little Press, 2013).

The theme of forbidden knowledge and how to obtain it goes back to Genesis and Prometheus and Greek tragedy. The human being seeks to know more than is useful, but somehow the attempt always fails and lessons of humility are learned, one way or another. This is also the story of the tragic genre, where pride must fail.

Strangely, if we admit there is magic in the creative, while we understand the cultivating of it, the mystery can remain inviolate in some way. Perhaps the oracular priestess is the one who truly believes in the oracle, while being accused of being fake. The best we can hope for is to be feared or suspected of fraud. My suggestion is that we embrace both the fakery and the fearful truth of the mysteries of writing. It is perhaps by way of doubt that we come to the truth, by way of humility that we come to prophecy.

Writing a book about creativity has the same risks. Someone once asked me, are you not muddying the spring? If creativity is a spring (see Chapter 5, 'Magic Portals'), then I would reply that I am simply clearing the path to the spring, ridding the water of what blocks or clouds it and even decorating the well, as is still done by some holy sites in England and elsewhere. There is always a mystery beyond us and we need to remind ourselves where fresh insight can come from.

The 'dirty word' aspect of magic and hence of writing then can be seen as a kind of fertility or a type of potency in ambiguity. The trick can achieve anything and writers can behave 'as Gods', if they have the intelligence to cherish the genuine insight and allow the world to decry their prophecy, in the knowledge that this is normal for the magic writer.

Characters from the history of magic, with their ambiguities of fakery and power, are usefully 'dirty' too, and great material for our creative work. Magic is, then, a dirty word, yet it has a glamour which is to do with real insight, found beyond the surface of the world.

Reputation, fame and solidity are perhaps for the kind of materialist person who does not realise that all human life is part inspiration, part skilful trick, plus suspension of disbelief and a tiny bit of the real magic of truth.

Write About

A serious magician who fails and is seen as a mountebank (itinerant quack who holds forth from a bench, or a charlatan).

A fake-seeming magician who rises to serious heights when his trick works.

A fortune teller revealed as a professor.

A genius who claims to be a fake, but is not believed.

The fertility or insight gained by being thought a fraud.

Finding a secret spring and clearing the mud away.

An 'evil' character who turns out to be good.

Magical Texts and Literary Examples

Magical

Cavendish, Richard. *The Black Arts* (1967); *A History of Magic* (1987).
Levi, Eliphas. *Magic* (1860; trans. 1913).
Rayner, J.H. *The Dairy of a Modern Alchemist* (1974).

Literary

Borges, Jorge Luis. *Labyrinths* (1964).
Frayn, Michael. *The Trick of It* (1989).
Hughes, Ted. 'Famous Poet' and 'The Thought-Fox' (1957).
Nabokov, Vladimir. *Pale Fire* (1962).
Thompson, Rupert. *Divided Kingdom* (2005).

2

Meeting the Magician

A meeting with a person who has magical qualities is, as with magic generally, an ambiguous experience. Such an encounter draws attention to the ordinary quality of the one who approaches and the danger of over- or underestimating the more powerful presence. This means that such an encounter is useful to all writers, because the relationship between the two, enlivened by the concept of some hidden power or superiority, can both show a quest for something stronger or better and highlight doubts and revelations. This book deals with ways of beginning, or pathways into the magic of writing and the meeting with someone who personifies that promise is a prime way that writers begin.

The ambiguity and controversy outlined in the first chapter are very much present again, especially when looking at the subject of meeting magicians directly. Again, these uncertainties are part of the fertile strength. One of the most useful and debated instances of meeting a magician in recent times is found in the writings of Carlos Castaneda (1925–1998), author of *The Teachings of Don Juan: A Yaqui Way of Knowledge* (1968) and many subsequent books. Castaneda was a student of anthropology, a subject much concerned with magic and its relation to Western thought, at the University of California, when his book was published. It is closely related to his PhD, as it is presented as a version of field notes and followed by a structural analysis of his findings. Initially the book was greeted with serious attention, but later commentators have questioned it as possibly being a work of fiction.

The assertion of veracity, via academic trappings, and the questionable elements of the story seem to me to be useful when thinking about writing such a meeting. They act as a metaphor for the ambition and for the slippery nature of the person who embodies the magical and might well be used by a writer. This might be done more self-consciously, but the serious dirtiness will add to your portrait and its longevity. Castaneda's work still raises many questions, doubts and hopes, as does his life after the success of the book – a notorious, even scandalous success which most creative writers can only envy.

The academic build-up to the meeting is important then, which can be seen as an echo of the beginning of *The Odyssey* for example, where we hear of the great deeds of Odysseus before we ever encounter him directly. Don Juan Matus, especially the Don Juan bit, seems an unlikely figure in some ways, to hold the massive influence ascribed to him. This, again, is part of the way of creating the magician for the reader. Don Juan has associations with past art, opera and stories of seduction on the one hand, and with being merely 'Mr John' in Spanish, the most ordinary of men. Greatness, again as Odysseus approaching his return to Ithaca, goes in disguise of the ordinary, while holding a secret.

When we get to Castaneda's actual meeting, we find the author waiting for a bus in a town on the border of the USA and Mexico. He is introduced by a friend to an old Native man with white hair, said to be someone who knows about peyote. The friend leaves them alone and silence ensues. The ordinary nature of the meeting is emphasised, as is the initial lack of communication.

Don Juan is seen as physically fit and, as Castaneda begins to babble about peyote, as if he knows all about it, he later feels he has been found out by the penetrating eyes of the silent magician. The fitness, despite age, and the gaze that looks through you are noticeable elements that emphasise the qualities of hidden power. Nothing remarkable is given away in this first meeting, marked by silences and politeness on the part of the magician and a naked eagerness to impress and to know more from the protagonist. All this takes place in the 'Introduction' and it is a year, we are told, before Castaneda really gets to know Don Juan and longer before he eventually becomes his apprentice. The suspension and build-up is worth noting.

One thing that is revealed is that Don Juan comes from a tradition of magic, that he had himself been someone else's apprentice. This passing on of the power adds weight to it, again in building up expectations. The reputation of the mage is another stage in the relationship, where we hear various tales, which might be true or not, of secret or even threatening powers. Several pages are devoted to this in the book. The next stage is accepting of the neophyte as an apprentice, which is done with nerves on one side and reluctance on the part of the mage. Don Juan agrees to notes, which are later to become something the mage mocks, but not to recording or photos, which would ring bells with those accusing Castaneda of fraud.

An acceptance needs to grow of things beyond the neophyte's normal experience, which builds up expectation of what is to be said, but offers a kind of glamour with its power as well as a kind of danger. With Castaneda, hallucinogenic plants play a part in this, as do other dangers, or promises of danger.

Simplicity and clarity are also emphasised, and a kind of new beginning, making the reader share in a kind of re-creation myth of the self. Don Juan, in Part One, begins by teaching Castaneda how to find a place to sit, which has semi-comic overtones, like a sorcerer's apprentice cartoon.

While listing the stages of meeting here, it feels as if we might be joining in the mockery, but this is not my intention. The significance of such a meeting is that it does represent a kind of creation myth, where a character can be defined and redefined and where the figure of the magician can offer education which allows real growth and development. Its use to writers as a motif is undeniable. Using the word 'neophyte' with its meaning of 'newly planted' suggests growth, as well as having religious connotations. These roles are significant and archetypal.

The main debunker of Castaneda seems to have been Richard de Mille in *Castaneda's Journey* (1977). De Mille might not be considered an uncontroversial figure himself, however. A nephew of Cecil B. de Mille, the great creator of film fantasy, Richard de Mille was a scientologist. His comic, clever debunking tone, where he almost seems to want to be Castaneda, is somehow part of the myth. It is worth noting that Castaneda wrote his first three books while still a student and that they were, at first, mostly acclaimed without ambiguity. Castaneda withdrew from the public world by 1973, a few years before de Mille's book came out and the mysteries surrounding the deaths of some of his followers revealed the ambiguity of the whole mythic cycle and its promise of truth and/or fakery.

On a personal note, it also seems, from de Mille's book, that a review from my undergraduate teacher and friend, Dudley Young (*New York Times Book Review*, 29 September 1968), caught the eye of a big paperback firm, who then created Castaneda's fame. Dudley (see Chapter 11, which quotes his book about Yeats) was not unambivalent about the book, however. It all adds to the magician's mystique.

If we look at Castaneda's book mythically, we might see parallels with *The Odyssey*, where the building up towards encountering the hero is similar. The writer and the reader seek to escape the ordinary world of everyday realities, where they have become blunted. Tennyson writes well of this in his poem 'Ulysses' (the Roman word for the Greek 'Odysseus'), when the hero in old age is 'an idle king/By this still hearth', thinking, 'How dull it is to pause ... // As tho' to breathe were life.' Joseph Campbell, in *The Hero with a Thousand Faces* (1949), in which he describes the stages of 'the hero's journey', would call this dull stage of readiness to meet some adventure 'common day'. His disciple, Christopher Vogler, in *The Writer's Journey* (1992; revised 1996) calls this stage 'The World of Common Day'. Meeting the magician can be taken as parallel with one of the next stages, 'Meeting with the Mentor'. With Campbell, this can also be 'supernatural aid', which could be a fairy godmother, or a disguised Goddess Athene, who appears to Odysseus' son Telemachus as Mentes, or Mentor, from which the word derives. Disguise, even trickiness, seems to be part of the archetype. Hermes is connected to alchemy and is the messenger of the Gods. This supernatural helper on a quest can be an old woman in disguise, which is a symbol of wisdom. The mentor gives you a gift or a charm often which has a connection, but most importantly gives you courage, as Vogler stresses in his section on the mentor; 'menos' means 'courage'.

Writers, like Virgil to Dante and Homer to Virgil, have mentors, who have taken the journey before them, but I would suggest that writers are mentors to their readers, as they take them to the encounter with the magic of writing. Literature as a form of encounter with a magician is a useful idea for writers. It is striking that an encounter with a magician from the nineteenth century, in a remote part of the county of Essex, in England, shares many of the motifs seen above.

Cunning Murrell (1900) is a novel by Arthur Morrison (1863–1945). Morrison, born in the East End of London, wrote his most famous novel, *A Child of the Jago* (1896), about the slums he knew well. *Cunning Murrell* is set in Hadleigh, near Southend, and is based on a character Morrison met. He wrote about his source in a journalistic article. The 'cunning' man behind the novel's reality is referred to in the dedication to the original publication, and a bit of folkloric material is quoted before the beginning of the novel. The reputation of the magician is there, as it is in Castaneda, as is the academic 'bigging-up' of the veracity of the story. The literary reference to evidence is there too, when the dedication refers to 'the amazing (and grimy) heap of documents'. This is reminiscent of Castaneda's notes, also a source of humour, but in his case against him rather than at the expense of the magician.

There is even a question of truth here, as the folklore quotation asserts that Canewden is sixty-two miles from Hadleigh. The folklorist must have been thinking of Hadleigh near the north Essex border, actually in Suffolk. This is fifty-two miles away, while Canewden, famous for witches, is in the marshes of Essex, only ten miles from the Essex Hadleigh, on the north side of the peninsula which has the Thames estuary to the south and the Crouch to the north.

It is worth looking at the beginning of the novel, where the encounter occurs, to note other points of comparison:

> The little old man presented the not very common figure of a man small every way proportionately. He was perhaps a trifle less than five feet high, thin and slight, but the smallness of his head and hands somewhat mitigated, at first sight, the appearance of shortness. Quick and alert of movement, keen of eye, and sharp of face, Cunning Murrell made a distinctive figure in that neighborhood, even physically, and apart from the atmosphere of power and mystery that compassed him about. Now he wore a blue frock coat, a trifle threadbare, though ornamented with brass buttons, and on his head was just such a hard glazed hat as was on Roboshobery Dove's. Over his shoulder he carried a large gingham umbrella, with thick whalebone ribs, each tipped with a white china knob, and from its handle hung

a frail basket. He nodded sharply to Roboshobery, who backed doubt-fully, made a feint of pulling at his forelock, jerked out "Good evenin'. Master Murrell, sir, good evenin'," and took himself off into the dark. For Cunning Murrell was the sole living creature that Roboshobery Dove feared, and it was Roboshobery's way not only to address the wise man (when he must) with the extremest respect, but to do it from a respectful distance; much as though he suspected him of a very long tail with a sting at the end of it. And he stayed no longer than he could help.

The atmosphere of the marshes plays a part here, these 'edgelands' comparable with the border town where Castaneda meets Don Juan. The local dialect again sees an emphasis on language difference. All this adds to the strangeness which creates expectation. Murrell is small but alert and 'keen of eye', while Castaneda feels that Don Juan sees through him. The slightly disguised fitness is there in both. The ordinary extraordinariness is part of the picture. Both men are old but vital. The introduction, by a mutual acquaintance, is again characterised by respect and rapid absence of the one introducing.

What is missing in Castaneda, although present in later commentators like de Mille, is the mocking, patronising tone Morrison uses. Ambivalence of feeling between the protagonist and the magician is a constant.

Creative Example

How I First Met Maggi C.

I was lost in an unfamiliar part of town, trying to find an address among the little older terraces out on the edge where mostly older, poorer people lived.

This was just after I'd split up with my girlfriend of nine years. I felt lost in life, as if I hadn't needed a sense of direction before. As a couple, we had drifted along well enough. Like many I suppose, I felt a need for action but had no sense of direction. The irony wasn't lost on me.

I noticed the big, old gas container, of the kind you hardly see now, still there on a bit of a scrappy grass hill and headed towards it for some reason.

About a week before, I'd seen by chance an old friend in the library. He was reading and making notes at a table when I went over. We had a whispered conversation, even though no-one else was in the room. I told him about my split.

He surprised me by asking if I'd ever seen a psychic. He said there was someone who he sometimes met in the library, a local chap who called himself a 'Psychic Life Coach'. It's not that we were entirely cynical about such things, as we'd both read serious stuff about the occult in the past, but we joked about the job description and about a book we'd both read at one time, on mystical self-help. Anyway, he found a card for this chap and gave it to me.

It was a few weeks later when I'd found the card again and phoned for an appointment.

Just around the corner from the gasometer was a woman's hairdresser, called 'Hair of Fortune', so I went in to ask, thinking the women who worked there would know who was around the area.

'Is there a psychic lives round here?'

'I knew you were going to say that,' one said, and we all laughed.

'That little alley opposite – number three,' another one said.

I hadn't noticed the alley, which comprised a terrace of six small houses. It wasn't the address I had, but I assumed I'd got it wrong.

A woman opened the door to my knock. She said 'Welcome'.

The door opened straight into her small living room. She wore a tweed skirt and looked of an indeterminate age. I stood there, as if immobile. She looked at me, seeming birdlike but somehow comfortable. A few seconds of silence, then I shuffled in, feeling dumb and out of place, but oddly reassured at the same time.

I handed her the card.

'Did he send you?'

'No, I ... he's not here?'

'He's about a mile away,' she said and laughed. Then, more serious, 'But I can help you.'

She asked me to sit. The chair was an old, brown plastic-covered armchair, scruffy but comfortable.

'Does he send people to you, then?'

She laughed again. 'Yes; ones he can't read or help.'

I found I was smiling. She made some tea.

I could see her through the door to the kitchen. She seemed younger than I'd thought and somehow brighter. She was lithe and strong looking, though small and dressed unfashionably. Something in me relaxed. I hadn't mentioned why I'd come.

Suddenly she began telling me it was good to be lost, even to feel abandoned. I sipped tea and she told me old stories of being lost in the woods and the world of the wood sharing all the possibilities of life to the abandoned one, in a series of tales within tales.

As she talked, the stories came to life and seemed to resonate all through me, as if I'd heard them before somehow, as if they were part of a shared past. I felt defenseless, but also helped at some deep level.

When she'd finished, she got up and began making more tea.

'If you're not lost, how can you be found?' she said, laughing a bit.

'I seemed to find my way here,' I said.

'Yes, you did.'

I asked her name as I left and she said 'Maggi C.' I thought I'd heard it before but wasn't sure if that was just the feeling I had from the whole meeting.

> Later that evening at home I'd looked for the mystical self-help book I'd once read and found a piece in it about storytelling that I remembered liking. It was extracted from a book 'now unavailable', as the note by the title said, and was by a certain Maggi C.

This story contains many of the elements noted above and listed below. Such lists are not to be taken too literally or even too seriously, in my opinion. Only take them seriously if they help you create an atmosphere of depth and needing to know what happens, of readiness to hear prophecy, which is another magic writers work. One benefit of such writing can be that it contains one or even two magically-aware characters, who can add reflection and depth to your work. Getting below the surface is the magical way of writing, in an age where this can be a problem, where current media encourage a surface-only culture, if we are not careful.

The 'active imagination' which challenges the self is in play in such meetings. The psychologist Jung in his *Red Book* (*The Red Book: Liber Novus – A Reader's Edition*, edited by S. Shamdasani, 2012) describes meeting 'The Magician Philemon', who usefully contradicts all his expectations, as a mentor should.

Writers can be mentors too, and therefore Gods in disguise, like the Homeric original of the name. This might be why writing classes with visibly successful writers are so popular, when they might be best just read closely, if we remember how significant texts are in this context. All us 'lost' Dantes seek our Virgil, our magic person to lead us from the labyrinth. Knowing these secrets, you can do this in your writing.

Ten Stages of Meeting the Magician

Academic/folkloric build-up.
Need of seeker/protagonist to leave ordinary world.
Appearance of magician: old, ordinary, even slight; but strong, hidden power.
Reputation of magician built up.
Eyes: keen.
Setting: borders (as Trickster) and strangeness of atmospheres/different
    class or language/dialect.

Silences and ambiguities/absurdities about relationship between magician
and neophyte, who also feels out of depth/uncomfortable/seen through.
Evidence of powers; simplicity; directness.
Texts involved.
Delay in revealing secrets.
Mentor parallel.

Names for Magicians and Protagonist

Magician:
Brujo (Castaneda)
Diablero (Castaneda)
Nagual (Castaneda)
Mage
Sorcerer
Sorceress
Enchantress
Enchanter
Thaumaturgist
Occultist
Adept
Mahatma
Seer
Shaman
Medicine Man
Witch
Warlock
Clairvoyant
Wizard
Wise Woman
Trickster
Mentor
Medium

Protagonist:
Seeker
Querent
Neophyte
Novice
Apprentice
Searcher
Mug (if writing comedy)

Write About

An encounter with someone who impressed you, turned into a magician by using some of the elements above.

Neophytes and mages: invent names and titles for magical encounters; then imagine the encounter.

Describe a magician in disguise and their transformation.

Write about an encounter in a patronising tone, the protagonist then being disabused and finally impressed.

Use the list of elements – use some, subvert some. Clever readers will have noticed eleven among the ten.

Create a comic meeting, then rewrite as serious, or a combination of both.

Seek out/look up the songs 'Nature Boy' by Eden Ahbez, 'Fool on the Hill' by the Beatles and 'Waiting for the Man' by the Velvet Underground and see how far they work as 'meeting a magician' texts. Create a song lyric which contains something you admire about a powerful person.

Look up some interviews with reclusive rock stars and see how much they parallel 'meeting the magician' motifs; then invent such a meeting in a creative work.

Create a fictional magical text and its author, whom you seek.

Research a magician from history and create an imaginary meeting with them. For example, Trithemius (1452–1516).

Magical Texts and Literary Examples

Magical

Carlos Castaneda. *The Teachings of Don Juan: A Yaqui Way of Knowledge* (1968).
Joseph Campbell. *The Hero with a Thousand Faces* (1949).
Richard de Mille. *Castaneda's Journey* (1977).
Neville Drury. *Don Juan, Mescalito and Modern Magi* (1978).
C.G. Jung. *The Red Book* (2009).
Christopher Vogler. *The Writer's Journey* (1996).

Literary

Songs listed in 'Write About' section.
Carlos Castaneda. *The Teachings of Don Juan: A Yaqui Way of Knowledge* (1968).
Ursula le Guin. 'Chapter 1' in *The Other Wind* (*Earthsea* series) (2002).
Arthur Morrison. *Cunning Murrell* (1900).

3

Magic Words

As we are creatures of language, self-created by words, it is easy to forget how powerful they are, as we take this extra dimension for granted. If we think of something powerful that someone has said to us – a declaration of love, or of hate; a word of encouragement or a curse of discouragement – and realise how that could change a life, we might begin to reawaken our sense of the power of words, or of words of power. The philosopher Wittgenstein said, in his *Tractatus Logico-Philosophicus* (1922), 'The limits of my language mean the limits of my world' (5:6). What he meant was that language has its limits, but looked at from our point of view, from the point of view of the writer, the power of language to define us is also called on strongly here. A word can make a world and a word can make a world of difference.

Writers love words and attending to words is part of our craft. We aim to set words against each other in a way that releases their energy. The histories and meanings of words and their shifting energies tend to obsess writers. There is the right word, 'le mot juste'. Many writers I know are lovers of dictionaries and I am no exception. If you study at a university, chances are you will have the complete *Oxford English Dictionary* available online. If not, ask your head librarian why not. The history, uses and instances of a single word are like a deepening of its power. My own favourite word-book is Eric Partridge's *Origins* (4th edition, 1966), which is an etymological dictionary, where he links related words together, as well as providing the history of their use. Partridge wrote many books on words, all of which are worth reading.

Writing, for a preliterate culture, must have seemed like magic. Symbols turn into real meaning and have power. Writing is said to have been invented to keep accounts, but the priests were not far behind and the poets with them. We are ruled by words still in the official document, the passport, the password, which once seemed a game or a magic word, but now is the difference between being part of the world and being excluded from it. The world of keeping count seems to want to steal the power of words from us or back to itself, but it is the magic of words with which we seek redress.

So it is easy to forget what we do when we write. We are using the tools with which the world is created to create a world of our own. So writing itself becomes a magical act, with moral potential built in. We are making spells, invocations, enchantments, curses and prayers. We are creating ourselves, or recreating ourselves and the world around us. Being aware of the power, of the potential, is something we must strive towards, if we want our writing to have energy.

We all have our favourite words or phrases. Actor and writer Robert Hill used to love the phrase, he told me, 'Circles Command', which sounds mystic and significant, until he realised it came from *The Highway Code*, which he had read before taking his driving test. As a writer he had noticed its resonance and potential, which was amusing but instructive about how a writer attends to such things.

Words can become dead to us and that is why we play with them and create with them, to reanimate their energy. Black magicians, it is said, reverse words to challenge their power. We make anagrams and palindromes and many other games of words to do the same. If you make a comic anagram of someone's name, or invent a secret nickname for a figure of power, you take some symbolic strength from them.

We can easily become sick of words, especially when overwhelmed by those bad magicians of words in the advertising industry or in the corporate business industry of self-justification, which all rings so false. The way the words ring to us makes a bad spell that we feel we must resist. You can become word-sick. Writers fight back against dogma. The word 'dogma' means both a principal laid down by the authority of a church and a kind of arrogant statement of opinion, as if it were gripping on to its owner like an aggressive dog, or as if it were saying it was God, if read backwards: 'am god'! It is worth remembering that both Jesus and Socrates, two of the most influential thinkers, did not write anything. They were written about, but their own selves remained fluid.

The uncanniness of words should not be underestimated. One thing that can make us aware of this is the use of the riddle, where the word at the centre of the words is hidden. With a riddle, there is also not always one answer, at least in the best riddles. In *The Exeter Book*, some of the oldest riddles have still never been solved definitively, which is great and extraordinary too. Kevin Crossley-Holland says, in the introduction to his *The Exeter Riddle Book* (1978), which derives from *The Exeter Book* (*c*. 975), 'The business of naming began with creation; the business of deceiving followed soon after, in the Garden of Eden. It is reasonable to suppose that as soon as man had wits, they delighted in riddling.' Because riddles have a surprise in them, by deceiving they give the word or subject depth and resonance. Like any writer, the riddler seeks to wake the word up, or wake us up to the word. Wrong answers are interesting, and can be right in a different way, and right answers are like finding a key. Here are three riddles:

Creative Examples

Riddle One

When you touch me I get unhinged
and I speak in silence
I can live longer than you
I can rest longer than you
I can travel with you easily
I can stay at home in stillness for years
Like you, I do not like the damp
and my back may be broken
and like you, when old, I can end up
in a Charity shop
You tend to judge me
and put your judgements on my back
I can baffle you or illuminate you

Riddle Two

Some think it doesn't exist but it can seduce you
It plays with your expectations
When you see something you didn't see before
When power is felt and time is contradicted
When mirrors and miracles move the mundane
Or when children want to be entertained
You use its name in vain

It has to be always beyond you
And never really respectable

Riddle Three

I am a word but what word?
I create as I speak
I might seem meaningless but I have power
I am like an alphabet start
and a palindrome
but I am not one of either

They used to write me over and over
around the walls in Roman times
but who am I?

There are two easy ways of approaching writing a riddle, which are levels on which they work. The first is an object described in action, abstractly, and/or personified. The other easy way would be to describe an abstract described as a person, or as an object. So if we had a bedside light as a subject, we could say it shines on one helpfully (in action), provides illumination (abstractly) and leans over our shoulder in a friendly manner (personified). If we were writing about the subject of love, we might say that 'I' inhabit two people who are close (personified), or that everyone says this is the one item they need when getting married (objectified). Read some riddles, especially those in *The Exeter Book* and see how they do it. The disguise reveals the inner aspects of the hidden subject and twists the mind to think deeply and metaphorically, which are all good training for the writer.

Mistakes are fun too. Riddle One was guessed as a suitcase once (answer = book). Riddle Two was guessed as debt, ego, love, light and power. The more ambiguous it is the better, I think, because that makes you think about ambiguity and how you might use that to deepen your writing (answer = magic).

Riddle Three was baffling to my students, especially if we had not mentioned magic words (answer = abracadabra). This word seems to come from the Aramaic for 'I create as I speak', as used in the riddle. It was favoured by the Romans and Gnostics and sometimes presented as a triangle amulet. Here, you write the letters of the word, gradually taking one letter away, to create a triangle, which also reads 'abracadabra' from the bottom upwards to the right. These days this magic word is used as an ironic joke, or by stage magicians, and might even be considered corny by them, but it is not without power.

We are publicly sceptical about magic words, but behind them lingers a sense of the true power of words which writers also know, as part of the links between magic and writing in the long tradition. The idea of 'the true tongue' lingers here, where words are really the names of the thing they represent and saying the word is equal with creating it, as in 'abracadabra'. The idea that we have lost this, lost the capitalised Word, for the lower-case sign disconnected from its reality, as linguistics seems to suggest, is a well-known idea in magical thinking. Thus 'the true tongue' is 'the lost tongue ... Can everyday words suffice to name the invisible? Or must they be used in a new way, according to rules, as the Cabbalists or surrealists believed?' This is from Andre Nataf's *The Wordsworth Dictionary of the Occult* (trans. 1991; 1994), in his entry on words. 'Lost speech relates to the myth of origins and refers to the world in a "psychocosmic" state where being coincides with knowing and words with the things they describe', as he says in a section called 'The Lost Speech'. Thus all writers seek this kind of harmony with creation; we want our words to seem both true and inevitable. 'Lost speech may even have been a form of telepathy', he adds.

Riddles, so common in all history and literatures, seem to come from the same source. As Kevin Crossley-Holland says in his Introduction to the riddles, 'the word "riddle" seems to derive from the Old English *raedan*, to advise, to council, to guide, to explain ... it presents the old in new ways'. Riddles, like the need to recover meaning and true words, seek to renew the language, to reanimate the tongue.

Naming is a significant act, as writers of fiction will tell you. Names tends to come from outside and are a non-material gift, usually from your parents. They connect you to something and have a power within you and over you. In a name, we have an idea of the power of words. A nickname will stick and can stigmatise you. One thing advised by 'new age' magical books is to add to your name something which you lack. A new name that means a quality you need will bring you the power and perhaps people do that to their children, such as giving the name Grace. Books of names and their meanings sell well, which means that at this level we acknowledge the power of naming still.

A spell is a saying which has the power of magic in it. The word 'spill' has roots in Icelandic or perhaps Gothic, meaning a saying or a fable. So a spell can be a kind of story. Spells can protect, attack, address a taboo or create an effect. They share many qualities with the prayer. We still use the word to describe creating an atmosphere, or a persuasive suspension of will to an outside source. There is something in the mantra-like repetition of words which is there to suspend meaning, or to allow a kind of state where a truer insight is revealed. The words of spells are then sometimes nonsense, or words foreign to the culture using them. So they can enhance meaning and transcend it, perhaps even at the same time.

This kind or paradox or process is a familiar feeling thing to those studying creativity and magic. A blessing or lullaby depends on the sound and the intonation, even the presence of the person giving it, but the resonance is still made from the power of the words and their clear intention. The Egyptian God of words, Thoth, was said to offer words that protected against evil, and protective spells are present in prayers, as well as lullabies and blessings. Thoth gave the words with which the Gods bespoke the world into being, as spells of this kind do, making it safe to trust by the invocation of security. He also protects the dead on their journey into the afterlife.

Spells that forbid can be of the 'Thou shalt not' commandment variety, where the repetition is again part of the power. 'My mother told me I never should/Play with the gipsies in the wood', begins a traditional rhyme, which has a compelling rhythm to add to its taboo sense. When we hear the word taboo, we know it means something important or full of potential, as well as danger, where a taboo can be something special or of special significance.

Spells for some specific aim, like love, can also be a good exercise for a writer to give their characters' desires full flow. The last pages of James Joyce's *Ulysses* (1922) contain Molly Bloom's monologue or stream of consciousness, created without paragraphs or full stops or other punctuation but perhaps punctuated nevertheless by the chorus, or mantra-like use of the word 'yes'. This sensuous and tender long prose poem is thereby like a spell and has often been read aloud or re-used in some way, for example by the singer and songwriter Kate Bush. The elevated literary use of language, even of experimental literature, partakes of the world of the magic spell.

A magical encounter, which seems to encapsulate the older power of magic and of spells and words against a more brutal rationalism, took place when the Romans were encountering the ancient British. Tacitus reports in his *Annals* XIV (available on the Internet Archive) about the Roman army encountering the Druids on the island of Mona (Anglesey):

> On the shore stood the opposing army with its dense array of armed warriors, while between the ranks dashed women, in black attire like the Furies, with hair disheveled, waving brands. All around, the Druids, lifting up their hands to heaven, and pouring forth dreadful imprecations, scared our soldiers by the unfamiliar sight, so that, as if their limbs were paralyzed, they stood motionless, and exposed to wounds. Then urged by their general's appeals and mutual encouragements not to quail before a troop of frenzied women, they bore the standards onwards, smote down all resistance, and wrapped the foe in the flames of his own brands. A force was next set over the conquered, and their groves, devoted to inhuman superstitions, were destroyed. They deemed it indeed a duty to cover their altars with the blood of captives and to consult their deities through human entrails.

This extraordinary scene, with the wild women in black waving torches and the Druids calling down curses on the invaders seems to show the Welsh in contact with the power of words and of spells. They caused paralysis and it was only the tyrannical discipline of the Romans which allowed them to prevail over the females and what they must have thought of as fanatics. Tacitus describes the natives as 'inhuman', while the natives seem all too human to us, depending on the old powers of magic against the military machine-minded Roman army. It also seems a familiar story of the ordinary against the tyrannous, the 'superstitious' against those who claim rationality but must have seemed to embody a kind of inhuman evil to the conquered.

What is not in doubt is that the natives believed in the power of magic and of their 'imprecations', which means their calling down of power to help them. We still have faith in words, as a single 'yes' or 'no' can change our lives, but we are in danger of becoming a tribe who forgets this, as we take too much for granted and deplete our power to those with power over us. Pre-writing societies had memories which went back dozens of generations, but we need to remind ourselves to renew our powers of calling down the energies into our writing.

During the Second World War, magic words were said to have been used by order of the government to prevent invasion. If this is true, this time it worked. In *The Book of English Magic* by Philip Carr-Gomm and Richard Heygate (2009), they report a repeating of 'You cannot cross the sea!' by magicians and the involvement of fire, as with the Druids. Some witches were also said to have used 'Go Away powder'. Even if this is fictional and farcical, it has echoes of power and of acknowledging the challenging power of words. The novel *Lammas Night* by Katherine Kurtz (1983) is based on this story.

We challenge the power of words too, when we see through politicians' spin. When business people play 'Bullshit Bingo', they do the same. This involves going to a conference or meeting and preparing in advance a sheet of clichéd business-speak phrases, which the participants secretly tick off as they occur. The cry of 'Bingo!', seemingly unconnected to the proceedings, triggers a power against the prevailing bullshit. This is a magic reversal of power being misused and here the rebel business people are connected with their Druid past.

The writer sees the power of words used, misused, neglected or elevated all around and tunes in to what works, what brings writing alive, to paralyse or to animate, to arrest or bless the mind of the reader.

Write About

A word connected with writing, turned into a riddle.

Choose a word you find special, a favourite or powerful one, then research its history and its usage (in etymological and quotation dictionaries, etc.), then write about its shades of meaning, its sound, its history. For example, the word 'doom' has many pages devoted to it in the full *Oxford English Dictionary*.

Getting someone to say your name, so that they acknowledge your existence.

A blessing, lullaby, or spell of protection.

Research Thoth and write a spell to get the help of this Egyptian God of words.

Write some comic commandments for being a writer: 'Thou shalt not ... '

Write a repeating monologue that seeks to persuade someone or seduce them.

Write a spell for a writer setting out on a piece of work, to bring flow, luck and so on.

Rewrite Tacitus from the Druid's or the wild women's point of view, creating the chant with which they paralysed their enemy.

Create a version of 'Bullshit Bingo' for a subject familiar to you.

Magical Texts and Literary Examples

Magical

The Exeter Book.
Philip Carr-Gomm and Richard Heygate. *The Book of English Magic* (2009).
Dion Fortune, *The Magical Battle of Britain: The War Letters of Dion Fortune*, edited by Gareth Knight (1993).
Andre Nataf. *The Wordsworth Dictionary of the Occult* (1994).
Lewis Spence. *The Encyclopaedia of the Occult* (1994).
Tacitus. *Annals*, XIV.

Literary and Words

Kevin Crossley-Holland. *The Exeter Riddle Book* (1978).
James Joyce. *Ulysses* (1922).
Katherine Kurtz. *Lammas Night* (1983).
Oxford English Dictionary (full edition).
Eric Partridge. *Origins* (1966).

4

How to Make a Poet: Rituals to Turn You into an Inspired Writer

Write About

Try this exercise before you read this chapter. Invent a ritual which turns someone into a writer. See later if there are echoes in some of the stories which follow (more exercises later).

Robert Graves' *The White Goddess* (1948) mentions the legend of Cadair Idris in Chapter 5 of his book about poetic inspiration and 'the language of poetic myth', as he says in the foreword. 'Cadair' means chair and Idris was the giant who sat there on the mountain, in his stone chair, to practise his astronomy and compose poetry, as he was skilled at both these arts. Cadair, or Ceder, Idris is a mountain in Wales, near Dolgellau in Gwynedd, at the south end of Snowdonia National Park, very popular with hikers and tourists.

The chair itself is said to be made up of the peak, plus two other features of the mountain, the saddle (Cyfrwy) and the lesser summit, Tyrau Mawr. So one may not sit in it as the giant did, though it seems big enough for many poets.

Because of the poet-giant, the legend has it that anyone spending the night on the mountain will be, in the dawn, 'dead, mad, or a poet'. Graves quotes a poem of Taliesin, the legendary Welsh bard who has a ritual all his own, which says 'I have been in the uneasy chair/Above Caer Sidin/And the whirling ground without motion ... ' All this speaks of the ambition and ordeal, the absurd magical scope of poetry.

The White Goddess remains a controversial book, but is full of insights about magic and creativity in its explorations of the Goddess of seasonal or cyclic inspiration. In Chapter 1 Graves talks about the themes of the book and the role of the poet. The book, he says, is about 'birth, life, death and resurrection of the God of the Waxing Year'. This God battles with the God of the Waning Year for the love of the White Goddess. 'The poet identifies himself with the God of the Waxing Year … the rival is his blood-brother, his other self, his weird.' He relates this eternal, cyclic story with a biblical quotation which A.E. Housman favoured about writing poetry: 'Whosoever shall seek to save his life shall lose it; and whosoever shall lose his life shall preserve it' (Luke 17:33). This kind of humble submission to the unknown is part of the poet's task then, as echoed in the earlier verse (17:25), after Jesus has cured the lepers. When he says, 'But first he must suffer many things, and be rejected of his generation', he is talking of himself, as well as those wishing to follow him. Losing yourself in order to be found echoes the poet on the 'uneasy chair'.

Housman's *The Name and Nature of Poetry* (1933) insisted on poetry being outside the measurable nature of our normal ways of thinking: 'Meaning is of the intellect, poetry is not.' Graves is at pains to talk of 'gleemen', who are court poets, being unconnected to the great 'Theme' of birth and death and renewal with which the true poet is concerned. The risk-taking of the chair ritual reminds us that writing with real depth can never be a safe activity.

Graves' book, first published in 1948, bursts with insights and connections about poetry and about the universal language of myth. Another book with a similar reconnective agenda is Joseph Campbell's *The Hero With A Thousand Faces* (1949). In the aftermath of two world wars, it was as if these two writers – one a poet, one an academic – sought to ask what it was, at base, human beings had in common and what it might be that we could use to reconnect ourselves at a deeper level. For this reason, both still seem vital templates for an attempt to link our inspiration to our lives, which reminds us of the task of the poet, according to Graves.

Achieving an optimism out of disaster is not a small theme. In Graves' poem 'The Haunted House', he speaks of a poet being called on to sing and the poet railing against the fools who ask, as he only has horror to tell. Yet the poem is a triumph of protest which begins to contradict its own agenda, as it is full of poetic energy.

Graves also had a positive effect on unlikely writers who visited him in Deya on the Spanish island of Mallorca. I heard Alan Sillitoe, author of *Saturday Night and Sunday Morning*, about working in a Nottingham factory, saying it was the exiled Graves who advised him to go where the life in his writing was and write from his own experience. This led directly to his success. Kingsley Amis similarly sought out Graves, although a very different kind of writer from the older poet. He still has much to say to us about truth and inspiration, in all his work.

The struggle of the 'uneasy chair' and the sacrifice for the Goddess are the way to make a true writer. The true writer must both confront and transcend the self.

The second way to make a poet is via an underworld ordeal, as described in the 'border' ballad poem 'Thomas the Rhymer'. This was a real person, who can be researched, but his journey in the ballad's tale, which makes him an adherent to the truth, is what concerns us here.

The definitive collection, or compilation of ballads, was made by a nineteenth-century American academic, the Reverend Francis James Child, where he put together over three hundred ballads in an enormous book. Ballad metre is a seemingly simple form and many of these, including 'Thomas the Rhymer', conform to this basic pattern of a four-beat line, followed by a three-beat line, in quatrains, the second and fourth lines rhyming. What is remarkable about ballads is their swiftness of action and their scope, their drama and magical elements. It is worth listening to some great modern interpreters of ballad, such as Martin Carthy, June Tabor and Pete Morton on his album of traditional songs, *Trespass* (1998). Avoid the Steeleye Span version of 'Thomas the Rhymer', though, and see if you can find an unaccompanied version of the real words and tune, like the one sung by Ewan MacColl (*English and Scottish Popular Ballads: Child 1*, 1961).

Thomas encounters the Queen of Elfland, and he bows to her, agrees to kiss her and goes on his journey, riding behind her on her horse, till 'living land was left behind'. She emphasises that Thomas has to be silent while in Elfland, otherwise he will never get home. After seeing the wonders ('ferlies'), he can return but she gives him 'the tongue that can never lie'. He protests at this, seemingly at the fact that he must be a gleeman, in Graves' terms, selling and pleasing his public, but she insists on him becoming a 'true' poet, which reminds us that the poem begins with the words 'True Thomas'. It is clear that money and favours have no place in poetry.

This amazing story has echoes of other literatures but what is remarkable is how humorous the tone of it is, the whole thing a kind of seduction by the Muse, with lines like 'O see you not yon narrow road/So thick beset with thorns and briars?/That is the path of righteousness/Though after it but few enquires.' This is the first wonder he sees and it feels that his worldliness is being mocked. It is also one of the sexiest encounters with a Muse figure, with the kiss and the sharing of a horse ride. After she bids him 'harp and carp' (sing and play) with her, then kiss her, she says 'Sure of your bodie I will be'.

After these wonders, they wade through blood to the truth and he is gone seven years. He returns with green shoes, and with the truth.

Thomas the Rhymer (Child Ballad, number 37C.)

TRUE Thomas lay on Huntlie bank,
    A ferlie he spied wi' his ee,
And there he saw a lady bright,
    Come riding down by the Eildon Tree.

Her shirt was o the grass-green silk,
    Her mantle o the velvet fyne,
At ilka tett of her horse's mane
    Hang fifty siller bells and nine.

True Thomas, he pulld aff his cap,
    And louted low down to his knee:
'All hail, thou mighty Queen of Heaven!
    For thy peer on earth I never did see.'

'O no, O no, Thomas,' she said,
    'That name does not belang to me;
I am but the queen of fair Elfland,
    That am hither come to visit thee.

'Harp and carp, Thomas,' she said,
    'Harp and carp along wi me,

And if ye dare to kiss my lips,
    Sure of your bodie I will be.'

'Betide me weal, betide me woe,
    That weird shall never daunton me;'
Syne he has kissed her rosy lips,
    All underneath the Eildon Tree.

'Now, ye maun go wi me,' she said,
    'True Thomas, ye maun go wi me,
And ye maun serve me seven years,
    Thro weal or woe, as may chance to be.'

She mounted on her milk-white steed,
    She's taen True Thomas up behind,
And aye wheneer her bridle rung,
    The steed flew swifter than the wind.

O they rade on, and farther on –
    The steed gaed swifter than the wind –
Untill they reached a desert wide,
    And living land was left behind.

'Light down, light down, now, True Thomas,
    And lean your head upon my knee;
Abide and rest a little space,
    And I will shew you ferlies three.

'O see ye not yon narrow road,
    So thick beset with thorns and briers?
That is the path of righteousness,
    Tho after it but few enquires.

'And see not ye that braid braid road,
    That lies across that lily leven?
That is the path of wickedness,
    Tho some call it the road to heaven.

'And see not ye that bonny road,
    That winds about the fernie brae?
That is the road to fair Elfland,
    Where thou and I this night maun gae.

'But, Thomas, ye maun hold your tongue,
    Whatever ye may hear or see,
For, if you speak word in Elflyn land,
    Ye'll neer get back to your ain countrie.'

O they rade on, and farther on,
    And they waded thro rivers aboon the knee,
And they saw neither sun nor moon,
    But they heard the roaring of the sea.

It was mirk mirk night, and there was nae stern light,
    And they waded thro red blude to the knee;
For a' the blude that's shed on earth
    Rins thro the springs o that countrie.

Syne they came on to a garden green,
    And she pu'd an apple frae a tree:
'Take this for thy wages, True Thomas,
    It will give the tongue that can never lie.'

'My tongue is mine ain,' True Thomas said;
    'A gudely gift ye wad gie to me!
I neither dought to buy nor sell,
    At fair or tryst where I may be.

'I dought neither speak to prince or peer,
    Nor ask of grace from fair ladye:'
'Now hold thy peace,' the lady said,
    'For as I say, so must it be.'

He has gotten a coat of the even cloth,
    And a pair of shoes of velvet green,
And till seven years were gane and past
    True Thomas on earth was never seen.

Thomas's underworld ordeal has obvious parallels with Graves' chair ordeal, and the White Goddess.

Perhaps the best known myth of becoming a poet is our third way, the myth of Orpheus.

ORPHEUS (from *Lempriere's Classical Dictionary*, 1864), a son of Oeagar by the Muse Calliope. Some suppose him to have been a son of Apollo, to render his birth more illustrious. He received a Lyre from Apollo, or, according to some, from Mercury, upon which he played with such a masterly hand that even the most rapid rivers ceased to flow, the savage beasts of the forest forgot their wildness, and the mountains moved to listen to his song. All nature seemed charmed and animated, and the nymphs were his constant companions. Eurydice was the only one who made a deep and lasting impression upon the melodious musician, and their nuptials were celebrated. Their happiness, however, was short; Aristaeus became enamoured of Eurydice, and, as she fled from her pursuer, a serpent that was lurking in the grass, bit her foot and she died of the poisoned wound. Her loss was severely felt by Orpheus, and he resolved to recover her or perish in the attempt. With his lyre in hand he entered the infernal regions, and gained an easy admission to the palace of Pluto. The king of Hell was charmed with the melody of his strains, and, according to the beautiful expression of the poets, the wheel of Ixion stopped, the stone of Sisyphus stood still, Tantalus forgot his perpetual thirst, and even the Furies relented. Pluto and Proserpine were moved with his sorrow and consented to restore him to Eurydice, provided he forbore looking behind till he had come to the extremist borders of hell. The conditions were gladly accepted, and Orpheus was already in sight of the upper regions of the air when he forgot his promise, and turned back to look at his long lost Eurydice. He saw her, but she instantly vanished from his eyes. He attempted to follow her but he was refused admission, and the only comfort he could find was to soothe his grief by the sound of his musical instrument in grottos or in the mountains. He totally separated himself from the society of mankind; and the Thracian women, whom he had offended by his coldness to their amorous passions, or according to others, by his unnatural gratifications and impure indulgencies, attacked him while they celebrated the orgies of Bacchus, and after they had torn his body to pieces, they threw into the Hebrus his head, which still articulated the words Eurydice! Eurydice! as it was carried down the stream into the Agean Sea. Orpheus was one of the Argonauts, of which celebrated expedition he wrote a poetical account, still extant. [Many later poetic works are attributed to 'Orpheus']. [Other legends tell how] nightingales, which built their nests near his tomb, sang their songs with greater melody than all other birds. Orpheus, as some report, after death received divine honours, the muses gave an honourable burial to his remains, and his lyre became one of the constellations in the heavens.

In comparison with the other tales, the story of Orpheus seems more of a warning of the problems of being a poet, as much as how to become one. He is no ordinary person, of course, being half God with a nymph as his wife. The warnings seem about youthful talent and its frailty and an impossible test which his human part must fail. Tests from Gods always seem to rely on human weakness, which might even be part of what is strong about being human, inasmuch as being susceptible to change and reconsideration is an admirable quality the Gods do not possess to any great degree.

This paradox is at the heart of the Orpheus story. The poet must look back, must reconsider the wonder of the world. The self-consciousness of love is there in the love song, as the tale might suggest. Orpheus is humanised in his song of weakness, as Gilgamesh is in his great epic, by heartbreak. His dissipation, the scattering of his body, reminds us of an agricultural God's symbolic turning into seed for the next harvest, as in the myth of Dionysus, the Greek name for Bacchus. Could this be a triumph, where he has become all song? Perhaps Orpheus warns us of the extremes of life being the subjects for a poet: those of love, death and the solitude of the singer. All these are tests for the poet.

Our first tale is of an ordeal making a poet on the mountainside, the second is an underworld journey, while the third is a whole life of tests and the 'second death' of becoming a poet. In all three, poets are made by a tough test and going through a cycle of life and death, having an ordeal and symbolically experiencing death. There is an encounter with a Muse (the giant on the mountain, the Queen of Elfland) or Gods, a return journey from the extremities of love, death, truth and sadness, even of madness. There is a sense of being tested almost to destruction, making sure Graves' great 'Theme' is there.

An element of sacrifice is in all three. Orpheus sacrifices his love finally, Thomas his voice, to go through Elfland, and ultimately his non-true voice, the mountain poet his peaceful rest. This reminds us that to sacrifice means to make sacred, to make us one with the world, as if poets must become everyone, in order to scatter their seeds of song. There is a purification of purpose in these writers' symbolic tests.

Creative Example

Death of Orpheus Blues

It was a bad time for the blues
Yet we sang them together
It was a bad time for the blues
So we sang them forever

No woman is as powerful
As the one I lost
I almost sang her back
Now all I do is count the cost

Now my love's invisible
Yet I still can't let her go
wild women call to me
But I just tell them no

My love is just impossible
My children unexpressed
The son you never had
Is your strongest side suppressed

It's a bad time for the blues
But it's the only song I know
And when they come to get me
The whole world will go

When they come to get me
It'll be with dance and song
I'll be scattered to the four winds
And I know it won't be long

And when I'm dissipated
No comfort will I bring
My head will float down river
Continuing to sing

The thing that sings forever
Will always be the news
Always torn to pieces
In a bad time for the blues

(From *An Essex Attitude*, Wivenbooks 2009)

Poets and writers, then, are not born but reborn. Each must undertake an ordeal. As W.H. Auden said of W.B. Yeats, 'Ireland hurt you into poetry' ('In Memory of W.B. Yeats', 1940). Orpheus gains and loses the world in his song of universal hope and suffering. Writers are thus taught to be beyond themselves and pay the price for their vision, however unpropitious the time. The price for their vision is to know both the curse and the blessing of being possessed by the truth.

Write About

A new name, a gift of truth, or a choice which makes you a writer.

A machine to make a poet.

Get lost in your writing, in order to be re-found: write something uncharacteristic of your usual style/subject; poets try prose and vice versa.

Write about the energy needed to be a true poet in a difficult time.

Graves describes a 'kindling' as an introduction to an Arabic poem which seeks to create the right poetic atmosphere with 'luscious' language. Write a 'kindling' to create a poet.

Write a ballad about how you became a writer.

Write about someone showing you three 'ferlies' (wonders) which challenge you as a writer.

Write Orpheus as a positive story, where his ordeals and end seem good and worth it to him, in order to write well.

What, in your life, would you sacrifice to become a good writer?

Magical Texts and Literary Examples

Magical

Joseph Campbell. *The Hero With A Thousand Faces* (1949).
Robert Graves. *The White Goddess* (1948).
Lempriere's Classical Dictionary (1864).

Literary

Francis James Child. *The English and Scottish Popular Ballads* (1882–98).
Robert Graves. *Poems Selected By Himself* (1957).
A.E. Housman. *The Name and Nature of Poetry* (1933).
Ewan MacColl. *English and Scottish Popular Ballads: Child 1* (album, 1961).
Pete Morton. *Trespass* (album, 1998).

5

Magic Portals (Making an Entrance)

Magical ideas are themselves portals into creative power, so again we begin in this book to sense magic as various kinds of beginnings. Beginnings are portals into new works or new lives. Every piece of writing has its portal, its crucial beginning. As I once heard novelist and teacher Lindsay Clarke say, 'Beginnings are fateful'. My previous creative writing book, *Myth and Creative Writing* (2011), being about myth, dealt with the narrative and symbolic. Here, the intention is to go more directly into these concepts, as magic portals, which are ways towards creative power.

An idea or a piece of writing can then be a portal. More specifically, a sacred site, a particular place or location, can be a portal, but with a piece of writing or an idea, a portal can be abstract too. When I talk to my students about this topic, I ask them to think of a possibility for a magic portal and we go round the room and hear them or write them on the board. Here are some of those portal suggestions:

A place of creation or destruction; a volcano; breaking into a building; a whirlpool; falling through the floor; waking and sleeping; madness and sanity; drinking a potion; dreams; hollow tree; circles; airport scanner; mirror; a portrait; a frozen moment; a cave; water; a rainbow; a tunnel; a childhood place; a secret place; a mentor; music; a descent; a hill; an underworld; imagination; fairy ring; birth/death; drugs; an aeroplane window; a hole; a black hole; a disaster; the sea; a lamp; a stone; a university; a church; a hospital; an image; a maze; an ancient site; a library; an animal; a doorway; an entrance ...

At once we can see that these are ubiquitous in writing: the entrance, putting us into a trance, can entrance us into a place of significance. Probably the most simple but powerful version of a portal for writers might be the book. The hinged collection of pages not only is a wonderful technological invention, but has an opening as a cover, which we pull back like a door, exiting in the same way by an ending door on the other side, as it were.

Owen Davies, a professor who specialises in writing about magic and its history, says, in his introduction to *Grimoires: A History of Magic Books* (2009), that 'grimoires also exist because the very act of writing itself was imbued with occult or hidden power'. This was because the 'art of writing was largely the preserve of the *datu* or priest-magician', in the Batak of Sumatra, for example. He adds that books 'can be magical without actually containing magic', as the presence of the book was impressive enough, just as books are used now to decorate a film set and give an atmosphere of hidden or stored knowledge, full of potential, of the potency of powerful narrative or information, of imagination.

He points out the perceived power of the Bible. It is still sworn on and the most puritanical of Christians were known to use the contents for divination. It is easy to forget how powerful books can be. Hunting through a second-hand bookshop for a precious, rare or serendipitously potent book is a kind of magical journey.

The origins of the word 'grimoire' for a magical book seem to Davies to be a cross between the Italian 'rimario', or book of rhymes, and the French for a Latin book 'grammaire'. Books are worlds within worlds and retain their magic, even in this age. The internet is good for many things, but finding books is a very useful function it performs – in a counter-expectation of itself, the new technology supporting rather than supplanting the old.

The poet Edwin Muir's *An Autobiography* (1954) offers a story, in the first chapter, from his childhood about a grimoire with uncanny powers. His father told him of the 'Book of Black Arts' which was passed from person to person by being sold for a silver coin, smaller than was paid by its current owner. You needed to sell it to avoid the negative powers that might damn you if you still owned it at your death. His father says a poor girl once owned it:

> The servant-girl of my father's story tried every means to get rid of it. She tore it to pieces, buried it, tied a stone to it and flung it into the sea, burned it; but after all this it was still at the bottom of her chest when she went to look there.

She goes mad. This feels to me like a wonderful metaphor for the dark power of the imagination, and of writing itself and of what is written as a portal of all kind of potentials.

Almost any literary work can then provide a portal, as we have seen, but John Norris of Bemerton's 'Hymn to Darkness' (1687) gives us night as a most profound portal to, among other things, inspiration. He begins:

> Hail thou most sacred Venerable thing,
>   What Muse is worthy thee to sing?
> Thee, from whose pregnant universal womb
> All things, even light thy rival, first did Come.
> What dares he not attempt that sings of thee,
>   Thou First and greatest Mystery.
> Who can the Secrets of thy essence tell?
> Thou like the light of God art inaccessible.

This 'metaphysical' poet has struck the occult gold of mysterious darkness, which yet holds the potential for all light and all life in its 'universal womb'. The dark is an embodiment of all that is common, but full of mystery and a simple reminder of the strangeness of life and death.

In the final stanza he talks of night being also the place of prayer, of the human need to acknowledge the mystery as a kind of moral good. A 'Votary' is someone vowed to the service of God.

> But thee I now admire, thee would I choose
>   For my religion, or my Muse.
> Tis hard to tell, whether the reverend shade
> Has more good Votaries or Poets made,
> From thy dark Caves were Inspirations given,

> And from thick groves went vows to Heaven.
> Hail then thou Muse's and devotions Spring,
> Tis just we should adore, tis just we should thee sing.

Religion and religious imagery seems to connect with the idea of a portal strongly, as the entering of a holy or sacred space. Gardens of Eden then, Utopias and their opposite are also portals. William Blake collects all these in 'The Garden of Love', from *Songs of Innocence and Experience*.

> I went to the Garden of Love
> And saw what I never had seen:
> A Chapel was built in the midst,
> Where I used to play on the green.
>
> And the gates of this Chapel were shut,
> And 'thou shalt not' writ over the door;
> So I turned to the Garden of Love
> That so many sweet flowers bore;
>
> And I saw it was filled with graves,
> And tomb-stones where flowers should be;
> And priests in black gowns were walking their rounds,
> And binding with briars my joys & desires.

Blake has an entrance and a place of transformation, both in the sense of potential renewal of innocence and in the way the garden has been transformed. Religion has lost its sacred place and become a prison, or it is both at once and therefore shows human potential to transform by the imagination, towards innocence or negative forms of experience. The lines between entry into a positive or negative portal are finely balanced and presented in a way which feels true to the ambiguities of the need to change and the difficulty of it.

Tom Chetwynd, in the entry on 'Place', from his *Dictionary of Sacred Myth* (1986) talks of the 'place of transformation' as being alchemists' 'images of the human body', like a room, a retort, a cup, crucible or other container. All are 'the fragile clay vessel of life', which is put under pressure by intensity or heat to effect the change. Thus the creative energy is called from the unconscious into light.

A house can stand for this transformative energy, as in Peter Ackroyd's novel *The House of Doctor Dee* (1993). In the first chapter, where he describes the protagonist approaching the titular, strange house, which looks a bit like a human figure, he writes, 'When I walked towards the steps, it was as if I were about to enter a human body.'

The image of water is a key one for a portal of transformation, as are the other elements of fire, earth and air. Water is used in baptism and the crossing of water symbolises change in many cultures. Water is also essential to us, part of us and where we see ourselves reflected, as Phil Cope points out in his book *Holy Wells: Wales* (2008). Health is associated with wells via wellness and water connects everything in its fluency and mutability. Cope says there are 'more than 40' holy wells in Wales alone. Included in the book are poems and one by Hilary Llewellyn-Williams addresses the well as a portal convincingly:

Hazel/ *Coll*

August 5–September 1

After last night's rain
light gathers on hazel leaves
with their three-clumped nuts,
and a wide-angled sun
shapes precise hills and stones.

I drag my hand through water.
Cresses stroke my skin,
which shrinks from their fleshiness.
I cup, and scoop to drink
what runs through my fingers.

A cold, sweet-metal taste:
water reflected on stone.
Myself reflected in water

shadowed and blurred, a dark
disturbance within the pool.

Tendrils of water spill down
inside me, tracing cool paths.
I splash my forehead and lids,
and wish for knowledge, for solid
sense, for a way through.

Knowledge and clarity
I need so much; I've let so
much slip by. In a hidden place
there's a well with my face in it
smudged silver, flickering,

and hazels growing thick
overhead; and there
my eyes look out from depths
of past and future, watching
the hazel ripples lift and spread.

Hilary Llewellyn-Williams: 'Hazel/Coll'
from 'The Tree Calendar', in *Hummadruz* (Seren, 1987) quoted with the
permission of Seren and Hilary Lewellyn-Williams

The poem, as it appears in the book about holy wells, is located at St Bruno's Well, Clynnog. The wishing and the washing, as well as the desire for 'a way through' here feel like experiences with which we can easily identify. The portal as a place of self-reflection is created through action and description, like a gathering of significance towards life being re-entered with freshness. Portals can, or must be, multidimensional.

Portals also bring to mind the whole idea of initiation and those who might help or hinder you as you are baptised or where the door is barred. The archetype of the 'Threshold Guardian' is important here, a figure who enables the entry or forbids it. We are familiar with these concepts from fairy tales, where a password might be required (now a distinctly non-magical element of everyday life).

Passwords mean a way in and are, as we know from our frustration with our digital machines, at times, maddening and frustrating. Edwin Muir, mentioned above in relation to magical books, has a good example of 'the horseman's word' in chapter one of his autobiography: 'the word which will make a horse do anything you desire if you whisper it into his ear', which you would pay another horseman any sum to tell you. Passwords remind us that we stand on a threshold.

The Roman God Janus embodies the Threshold Guardian, as he is often depicted with a key in one hand and a stick in the other, with two faces looking both ways at once. He could be the all-seeing writer, wielding his creative power, or an irritating reflection of the paradoxes of human nature when conflicted. Threshold Guardians represent or reflect all of the negative, or positive, aspects of your own unconscious mind. People learn to do this to each other too, so someone who enables or prevents you from entering where you need to go, or how you need to grow, can become the archetype. They are forces in the world as well as aspects of the self. They present or reflect your limits and your potential back to you. They are themselves the image of a portal, open or closed, to new life.

Death and birth and love, or 'Births, Marriages and Deaths', are the big portals we attend to. So from these primal life-events to the giving of an award, we enter little or huge underworlds, or dark nights of the soul, to rehearse our creative renewals. Your writing, your poem, your narrative, is your alchemists' retort.

Creative Example

The Reluctant Antiquarian

I was listening to my friend Maggi C discoursing about Stonehenge.

'There are as many ideas – druidical, scientific, tribal – as you can count ... '

Was 'druidical' even a word? 'Many' seemed to me the operative word. Too many cars, too many people visiting, theorising. The whole place, in the unexpected hot sunshine, seemed defined by 'too-many-ness' – which definitely wasn't a word.

The stones themselves were big and forbidding, layered over by bigness and by projections of secrets.

Maggi was asking me if I felt anything. She wasn't offended when I laughed. She just smiled and looked sunny. Her ability to reflect the weather never stopped amazing me. She was effortlessly positive. I felt guilty, but I didn't say that. How to tell her what I felt – that felt like a problem.

She was more intelligent, more sensitive than me and I liked that. She deserved more, her honesty, it seemed to me, demanded honesty from me in return.

'Too many people. Too many theories. Monolithic resistance – maybe I feel that.'

I couldn't help trying to make her laugh, and, bless her, she did just that. I was relieved when we left the viewing area and drove off to find a quiet tea shop somewhere.

A few weeks later, my heart sunk a bit when she suggested another outing. But it rose a bit too, as she was the best company, even if, mostly, I couldn't, metaphorically speaking, keep up.

The drive through Sussex was pleasant and fun, on our way to meet the Long Man of Wilmington.

'Just an excuse for a nice ride out, with a destination to keep our focus,' she said.

'I'm not used to being the sceptical one, really,' I said. I liked her mocking me a bit.

'I've got a present for you,' she said.

She could surprise me, but it felt like a happy, ordinary surprise, because with her, such things were not exactly expected, but not unusual.

'O, good.'

She opened the glove compartment and handed me a postcard. It was of Eric Ravilious' painting of the Long Man of Wilmington. As I glanced at it, I knew immediately that I was going to be moved and impressed by going where we were going and that I loved Maggi very much, so I told her these two things.

When we got there, we were the only people around and we walked about the footpaths on the Downs, approaching the figure from above, at first. There was a highness in the air and a lightness, the weather being as good as our last trip.

Eventually we got to where Ravilious must have stood to sketch or paint his picture.

The figure rose from the hillside, above the path that seemed to lead to it. It is a simple chalk outline of a standing man, holding two uprights apart in his hands. These are like poles, or an opening of some kind. It was an entrance, a gate, a measurement, surveyor's poles, a sentinel, a square, a space of life, or larger-than-life, a giant, a humble assertion of life. You felt like it might arrive, it might walk towards you, or invite you in, at once part of and separate from the landscape.

I tried to say some of this. Ravilious emphasises the pit or hollow of ground beside the figure, as if the Long Man had come from there, emerged or was always emerging into the light.

> There are many theories and debunkings about this figure, this place, too. None of them mattered to me as I felt a connection between us, standing there, seemingly casual, just looking.
>
> Maggi didn't really say much, except to say 'Yes' now and again, as I murmured my thoughts, without thinking about what I said at all. Something seemed to bounce in the air between us, seeming to lift us up like a new energy, as we walked back to the car.

All the energy in this story is intended to be in the *approach* to the portal, where the character of the protagonist and the need for change is portrayed. Of course, the parallel portal is the entry into love, as much as into the place or image.

Another aspect of the story, which can be useful for a writer, is having a character who is aware of the dimension they are seeking to add to their work. In this case Maggi C is *magically aware* and this gives the writing licence to foreground its magical elements. She is also a kind of Threshold Guardian, in that she leads the narrator into accepting the potency of location.

The Long Man himself seems to be a comment on entrances, as he stands on the down, or seemingly suspended in air, with his ambiguous gate or staves and in his movement or stillness.

You may notice in this chapter that I have avoided the direct entry into a magical world, which is the way many writers use a portal. The point is to demonstrate that the concept can be used in more ways than just an opening to fantasy. A good example of entry into a different, magical world is in the Guillermo del Toro film *Pan's Labyrinth* (2006). The alternative world here opposes the harsh background in which the film is set, so that the two worlds work synergistically, rather than the alternative being merely a passport to incoherence.

Probably the most famous literary example of a lost, once-glimpsed, brighter world is Alain-Fournier's *Le Grand Meaulnes* (1913), where an extraordinary house, come across by accident, where a fantastic party occurs, is never found again. Herman Hesse's *Steppenwolf* (1927, trans. 1929) famously has the challenging portal of a sign, reading 'For Madmen Only', appearing on doorways.

The writer stands at the portal, with instincts as much as intelligence alert, with the magic word to hand, opening the door of a page, writing a way into the magic of inspiration.

Write About

An approach to, an arrival at, and/or the appearance of a portal and the feeling of what might be in store for you (everything but actually entering in).

Create a first line that invites the reader in; or write several of these.

Invent and describe a magic book, which might have a power in itself, with its title, description and age, and reveal a small part of what you imagine is its content which is decipherable.

Write directly to a portal (as John Norris does to night), asking for its help to be inspired.

An element as a portal; a vessel as a portal.

Passwords return to magic.

A key moment from your life (perhaps childhood) as a portal.

Magical Texts and Literary Examples

Magical

Tom Chetwynd. *Dictionary of Sacred Myth* (1986).
Owen Davies. *Grimoires: A History of Magic Books* (2009).
Adrian May. *Myth and Creative Writing* (2011).
Phil Cope. *Holy Wells: Wales* (2008).

Literary

Peter Ackroyd. *The House of Doctor Dee* (1993).
William Blake. *Songs of Innocence and Experience* (1794).
Alain-Fournier. *Le Grande Meaulnes* (1913).
Helen Gardner (ed.). *The Metaphysical Poets* (1966).
Herman Hesse. *Steppenwolf* (1927).
Hilary Llewellyn-Williams. *The Tree Calendar* (1987).
Edwin Muir. *An Autobiography* (1954).
Guillermo del Toro's film *Pan's Labyrinth* (2006).

6

Tricksters

The last chapter introduced us to the Threshold Guardian archetype, but the one closest to magic, in its broadest sense, is that of the Trickster. This figure, hard to pin down, contains something of the fertile, fraudulent and creative paradoxes, as discussed in Chapter 1. Tom Chetwynd, in his *A Dictionary of Symbols* (1982), defines the Trickster as 'a figure who hovers on the border of conscious and unconscious, where the light and shadow play tricks'. The Trickster is linked with creation and destruction, absurdity, bodily folly and wisdom, extremity, sex, existential uncertainty, opposites – and shit! Linked to Dionysus, the God of wine and fertility, of spring and change, the Trickster personifies upset/revolution/disorder/down-to-earthiness, and ambivalence, uncertainty and the paradox of continual change. The most human of archetypes, the Trickster is the most likely to disrupt or embody human folly. The Trickster demands creativity, even, it seems, if it results in our destruction.

All magic is then Trickster matter, where life seems stolen from death and the eye and the hand deceive, in the quickness of life, in jokes and the fluidity of the imagination. The Trickster is linked to the Changeling, such as Thetis and Proteus, who could shape-shift at will. The Trickster is a life-shifter. Usually depicted as a male, he is vulgar, lustful, pointless, directionless, shocking, stupid, the victim, the liar, the cheat, the man who tells nonsense as sense. As Marina Warner says of the Genie, or Djinn, in the *Arabian Nights* (in her wonderful *Stranger Magic*, 2011), he is 'capricious'. He is all we do not like to think we are and he turns the world upside down.

Joseph Campbell, in *Primitive Mythology* (1959; revised 1969: chapter 6), makes no bones about it when he identifies this figure as God the Creator. The very trickiness of existence is implied in creation mythology, where the highest form of being is made from clay. 'We come from clay and we all go back they say/So don't chuck a brick, it might be your Aunty May', as the old song goes. Campbell uses the word 'culture-bringer', connected here to the idea of carnival, identifying the figure with the old European Mr Punch character, or with the Lord of Misrule, a figure brought from low to high society in the festive season, to upset the order of the world and let the wildness out in proper celebration of the promise of new life in the darkest time. The Trickster is all human folly, which, paradoxically, reveals all human strength, giving 'the character of topsy-turvy play to the feast', as Campbell says.

He is a hero and, like Loki, whose name means fire, or Prometheus, who tricks the Gods into giving humans fire, the Fire-Bringer to mankind. Metaphorically he gives us the creative aspect of God, which is our inspiration and potentially our undoing. He reminds us to be in awe of creation and not to think we, as humans, can ever own creation. Like magic itself, he can never be respectable.

Creative writing professor Lewis Hyde devotes a whole illuminating book to the archetype as essential to the creative: *Trickster Makes This World* (1998). In his introduction, he says,

> I want to argue a paradox that the myth asserts; that the original liveliness and durability of cultures requires that there be space for figures whose function is to uncover and disrupt the very thing that cultures are based on ... how social life can depend on treating antisocial characters as part of the sacred.

He echoes Campbell here, as when he talks of human vanity, or rightness, which can lead to 'unconscious cruelty masked by inflated righteousness'. This creator of life and culture then is strongly linked to comedy which always has a quality of inflating the small and deflating the overblown.

Despite the fact that we live in a world where the individual is encouraged to think of themselves as a clever maverick and that anyone might be a trickster, Hyde insists that 'our disruptions are not subtle enough' – we are too smug, too simplistic not to need to be undone.

The book that really introduced the concept to other writers on myth and magic was Paul Radin's *The Trickster* (1956), in which he studied the mythology of the 'American Indian' and helped define the term. In his 'Prefatory Note' he says that these stories of the Trickster are the oldest and most universal of myths, common to all societies and familiar in figures of the clown and the fool. The Trickster 'dupes others and is always duped himself'; also, he has 'no values' only 'passions and appetites' and is the source of the comic and the existential struggle. The archetype insists that we have to make ourselves out of our animal foolishness. Thus the Trickster seems to be the part of our shadow selves which breaks through to be against the norm, against our tendency towards stasis.

But the Trickster lives in stories. What are trickster stories like? They are often short and mad, with a kind of crazy logic. The central character is sometimes an animal, like a fox, or in Native American stories, the Coyote. Lewis Hyde starts with a personalised version of a tale Campbell also tells. This is one where 'Coyote' sees a man throw his eyes up into a tree in order to see further and gets the man to show him the trick. He is warned not to do it too many times, or his eyes might not return. But of course he does just this. He begs ill-fitting eyes from two passing creatures, one tiny and one huge and carries on.

Hyde imagines this story to be a lesson for him, as it was told to him by an American Indian who gives him a lift when a student. Was it something to do with him seeing everything, via his years of study and therefore about his vanity of learning? It is a good story, undermining and creating useful doubt and real thought.

The story of the Three Army Surgeons from Grimm's has a similar feel of the disruption of human vanity. It also fills some of the criteria for being a Trickster tale, inasmuch as the disruption turns back on the protagonists, as they threaten the order of their world. It shows a link between the kind of primal tales and our own era of science and medicine. The thing the story does not have is a Monkey, a Fox or a Coyote figure, however, although they fancy themselves as Tricksters nonetheless.

THREE ARMY SURGEONS who thought they knew their art perfectly and were traveling about the world, came to an inn where they wanted to pass the night. The host asked whence they came, and whither they were going.

'We are roaming about the world and practicing our art.'

'Just show me what you can do,' said the host.

Then the first said he would cut off his hand, and put it on again early next morning; the second said he would tear out his heart, and replace it next morning; the third said he would cut out his eyes and heal them again next morning.

'If you can do that,' said the innkeeper, 'you have learnt everything.'

They, however, had a salve, with which they rubbed themselves, which joined parts together, and they carried the little bottle, kept constantly with them. Then they cut the hand, heart and eyes from their bodies as they had said they would, and laid them all together on a plate, and gave it to the innkeeper. The innkeeper gave it to a servant who was to set it in the cupboard, and take good care of it.

We have a typically fast opening to a fairy tale, with the wandering, the boasting and the impossible already happening, as well as the challenge to the norm, even to the taboo of bodily integrity, as explored much by current science fiction. We also can feel something about to go wrong and that such vanity will be overturned.

Later, the servant girl opens the cupboard to feed her lover and a cat steals the organs, which the two replace with the hand of a hanged thief, the cat's eyes and the heart of a pig, recently slaughtered. Here we have the reduction to the animal essence wrought by appetitive. They later start acting like a thief, a cat and a pig and try to return and get back their organs, without success.

So while there is no one Trickster figure here (the cat, as saboteur?), some elements are obviously from the same archetype. *Aesop's Fables* is another Western source of tales which have something akin to Trickster myths. 'The Fox and the Crow', where the Fox praises the crow so that it drops a piece of cheese in answering the flattery, does not have the quality of real upheaval. However, in the tale 'The Ass, The Fox, and the Lion', the Fox tries to get the Lion to help him consume the Ass by trapping it in a pit, whereupon the Lion then consumes him, before bothering with the Ass. This then does approach the Trickster in the form of the Fox, because he is also the victim.

The creativity implied in the upheavals of the tales is paramount, as is the reminder of our human limits. The fertility of the essences of life is there in the paradoxes of imagination and human animal baseness. Lewis Hyde sees the Trickster in the artist and Aesop looks very much like a Trickster himself. He collected the tales, but he was also, so legend has it, a slave who was so ugly and offensive that others wanted to kill him by throwing him over a precipice at Delphi, where the oracle would give prophecy. These strange paradoxes, his fame and humble birth, his offensiveness and honour, make G.K. Chesterton wonder, in his introduction to the fables, if it was perhaps for being morally but correctly self-righteous that he was hated. The trickiness of the magic of creativity is present again.

Poet Philip Terry, in his *Fables of Aesop* (2006), has the collector of tales as a central figure in one of his extraordinary reworkings of the myths:

MORE TROUBLE WITH DELPHI

Hearing that Aesop continued to mock the citizens of Delphi, the priest of the oracle of Apollo once more summoned him to their temple. When Aesop arrived they bound him in chains at once, carrying him to the cliff from where he was to be thrown to his death. Aesop pleaded with his captors, but to no avail. As he was on the point of being thrown over the cliff, he told them the following fable. 'A man fell in love with his own daughter, and sending his wife away on business forced himself upon her. "Father," she said, "this is an unholy thing you are doing. I would rather have submitted to a hundred men than to you." This is just how I feel towards you, men of Delphi. I would rather drag my way through Syria, Phoenicia, and Judea than die here at your hands.' They threw him over the cliff to his doom. Landing with a bump in a thorn bush 200 yards below, Aesop cursed them, then picked himself up and began the long journey home.

Aesop is author of his own folly, by his insistence on the truth of his disruptive fables. Travelling is involved, as is his creative resilience. He lives, despite, or because of, his threatened death. So the liveliness of creativity is present too. The animal, and seemingly gentle quality of the original fables may not be there, but the Trickster element is in the foreground. The animals in fables are always archetypes or even stereotypes, but their fixity makes them strong and constant for symbolic use, which we still understand. G.K. Chesterton sums up the moral of fables as being the fact 'that superiority is always insolent'. This is the source of comedy and of tragedy and the Trickster tale at best does both.

It is worth noting that the beginning tales of 'The Winnebago Trickster Cycle' are ones which feature 'the chief' as the Trickster, in Paul Radin's seminal study *The Trickster*. As he later comments, the chief is reduced to nothing in the tales, becoming more and more absurd and breaking every taboo, 'emerging out of ... complete isolation and lack of all identity' (Part Three; V). Just as Philip Terry's Aesop has become an archetype for a writer, insisting on his truth, so the chief is depicted challenging all authority, doubly absurd as the authority is his own. To write as a Trickster is to challenge the self and its vanities.

Ted Hughes' collection of poems *Crow* (1970; 1972) is strongly associated with Trickster myth and its reception prompted Hughes to point this out in 'A Reply to My Critics' (*Books and Issues*, nos. 3–4, 1981). His poem 'Examination at the Womb Door' is a good example, as it has a classic exchange, a to and fro of fixed argument where death is the answer to all questions, apart from the exception of the living being – in this case, Crow himself. This, then, is the primal energy of any Trickster tale, where death is challenged at the most basic level to include rebirth, while nothing is left unchallenged and no extremity of thought or base level of existence put aside in any way. The poem is comic, ritual, absurd, potentially violent, exceptionally primal – which are all the things demanded from writers, you might say.

Hughes also saw Crow as an emblem of England and felt the need to attempt 'to bridge the culture gap that seems to render my poem *Crow* nearly inaccessible to some readers', in 'A Reply to My Critics'. The Crow poems are not 'Black Comedy', as 'Black Comedy is the end of a cultural process, Trickster Literature is a beginning'. He emphasises the 'nihilism' of Black Comedy, while 'in Trickster Literature the optimism and creative joy are fundamental'. This may be one of the fundamental problems of our time, for writers, who might be tempted by the pessimistic wallowing in the lack of meaning, while inherent here is a yearning towards the rebirth of comedy which the Trickster implies and which Hughes insists upon. We might think of tragedy as the superior medium, but comedy says that life goes on and the Trickster combines, at best, both.

The Trickster also offers, in its tale format, often short and sudden, opportunities for writers to cross or mix genres. Simon Armitage's collection of prose-poems, or fables, or flash-fiction even, called *Seeing Stars* (2010), is a good example. In the piece called 'My Difference', we seem to be in a creative writing class, where the norm is upset by a challenge to the norm of the abnormal being useful for creative writers. The protagonists' norm is too normal, perhaps. The difference of the protagonist is not extreme enough to please the tutor, but to the writer it is everything. This is about the artificial atmosphere which can be generated by the 'workshop', where subtlety can be subsumed to a norm, which is really the last thing someone creative needs. Armitage's tales are intellectually tricky, often featuring famous people as characters and dreamlike, where everything has turned into an archetype and every thought into something that needs to be disrupted by a surreal but just-seeming overturning, which ultimately feels right in their craziness.

A more straightforward Trickster is found in Shel Silverstein's poem 'The Perfect High', first published in *Playboy* magazine in July 1979. He describes a kind of hippie hedonist, trekking to Nepal to find a guru who lives on a mountain and who knows the secret of the perfect high of the title. The guru tells him it is in himself, but the hippie cannot accept this and becomes threatening. The guru tells him of a long quest to go on and sends him on his way. The poem concludes with the guru saying that people prefer rubbish to the truth. Is this a Trickster tale, though? Is the hippie the travelling border-dweller, who is fooling himself? The one who seeks, like Loki or Coyote, the limits of civilisation and therefore its definition? The fact that the tale raises these questions tells us that it, at least, transcends its black comedy of foolish seeking after pleasure. It has foolishness and wisdom closely aligned at its heart.

That the Trickster is universal is not in doubt. On a misericord (mercy seat) in a church in Lavenham, Suffolk, not far from where I live in England, there are two musicians with animal bodies, which seem to suggest a medieval form of a vulgar, surreal challenge to reality, or a revelation of secret energies. Another medieval picture I know depicts a fox dressed as a bishop, preaching to geese. Tricksters are embedded in our culture for writers to discover.

One Trickster tale, told by Campbell, has Coyote, continually saying he has control over his bowels, ending up buried in a pile of his own dung. The rude, baseness is part of the archetype and the return to earth vital in the element of creation myth which the Trickster calls upon.

Creative Example

World In His Hands

'Go, hands, and caress that lovely person,' said the Bogey-Man. They went.
  'Hands, come back!'
  They came back.
  'He's got the whole world in his hands,' he sang.
  Then he said, 'Go and grab that person's behind, that man's wallet and that woman's bacon sandwich. Did I say "handwich"?' And he laughed.
  But the hands could only do two things at once.
  'Come back, hands,' he said.
  They wouldn't come. One hand was stuck to a bacon sandwich and one was stuck in someone's pocket.
  Bogey-Man tore two pictures of hands from a magazine with his teeth and stuck them to his arms. He begged the person whose behind he tried to grab for forgiveness and that person gave him one back and told him to go to a second-hand shop and keep them to himself.
  The one hand went back to him and, on the other hand, eventually the other hand re-grew too, but looked thin, like a picture in a magazine.
  But at least he could use it to wave goodbye.

This is an attempt to use the Coyote, or Army Surgeons' model of bodily parts representing human appetite and about overreaching, especially in the case of the above, where extra puns add to the fun. Writers must experiment with how serious they can be in this form, without losing the surface of comedy and absurd appetite.

The writer is the Trickster, if we are to believe it and therefore a victim as well as a creator in their own magic trick. Our tales must challenge and surprise us and give us a sense of edgy danger, in order to risk the creation of something really new or renewed against the dark energies of destruction, which are also those of creation.

Write About

Someone who symbolically loses part of their body (which has psychological significance) through overconfidence, but manages to get it back partially, or by luck (as in the "Creative Example" above).

Find an old Trickster tale (from Loki in Norse mythology, or from Native American traditions, or elsewhere) and rewrite.

Start with something in your own life which has a crazy logic and let that sense flow towards a new story, with wilder invention. Then edit into something which holds some of the Trickster motifs of challenging perceived superiority.

Create a clever animal or new being, like a mythical animal, which might make the protagonist of a Trickster tale.

A writer of Black Comedy keeps on failing. Paradoxically, as his work gets funnier and more and more resilient, the darker it gets, in true Trickster style.

Invent a female Trickster, perhaps like Shahrazad who weaves tales to stay alive in the *Arabian Nights'* frame story, but more challenging.

Imagine a Green Man as a Trickster and tell a tricky tale of spring.

Magical Texts and Literary Examples

Magical

Joseph Campbell. *Primitive Mythology* (1969).
Ted Hughes. 'A Reply to My Critics' (1981).
Lewis Hyde. *Trickster Makes This World* (1998).
C.G. Jung. 'On the Psychology of the Trickster Figure' (1954).
Paul Radin. *The Trickster* (1956).

Literary

Aesop's Fables. Introduction by G.K. Chesterton (1912).
Simon Armitage. *Seeing* Stars (2010).
Ted Hughes. *Crow*. 'A Reply to My Critics' (1981).
Shel Silverstein. 'The Perfect High' (1979).
Philip Terry. *Fables of Aesop* (2006).

7

The Tarot

In the original version of John Fowles' novel *The Magus* (1966), he quotes from *The Pictorial Key to the Tarot* (1911) by A.E. Waite, using Waite's description of the first card of the major arcana of the tarot cards, which is The Magus, or The Magician. The major arcana are the extra cards in the tarot deck and that which emphatically differentiates tarot cards from conventional playing cards. 'Arcana' means a place of containment or safe-keeping and these cards have been referred to as Trumps Major, as Waite does, quoted by Fowles.

This card obviously links with the last chapter, in that The Magus, both in the card and in the novel, is a Trickster figure, although the major arcana also includes a card for The Fool, which would correspond to The Joker in normal playing cards. The Magician card, however, can sometimes be seen as the beginning symbol of a progress through the archetypes these twenty-two cards represent, and hence an apprentice mage, a beginner on the magical path. Often, he is a young man, holding a wand, as if beginning to practise his art.

In the revised edition of *The Magus* (1977), the description of the card is absent, but the author's Foreword talks of the work itself as being 'a first novel', saying that the revision was partly because of this, as it needed 'stylistic' attention. So, while the description of the card from whence he got his title is gone, the resonance with the author as apprentice mage seems stronger. When looking at the 'thematic and narrative' contents, they are much the same, as he says. The novel deals with a young and naïve man being confronted with magic and going on a journey through some major archetypes of life via a mysterious central character who seems to be leading him through these stages. It is as if Conchis, the magician who is intent on teaching Nicholas, the young protagonist, represents card 21 of the major arcana, The World. This is the card of completion, of full integration of the conscious and unconscious.

Waite's description of the card does not mention the beginning of magic, or the youth of the figure as depicted in card 1, but the resonance is there between Fowles' two characters, as if both are versions of the same thing, with the progress through the archetypal cards a hidden structure of the novel. The Magus is then the beginner and the one who teaches magic, as in cards 1 and 21.

The writer as always beginning and striving for completion will be familiar to readers of T.S. Eliot's poems: 'Every phrase and every sentence is an end and a beginning' ('Little Gidding' V). Famously, Eliot mentions the Tarot in *The Waste Land*, particularly the card called The Hanged Man. With card 0, The Fool, and card 1, The Magician, The Hanged Man is probably one of the closest cards to the archetype of The Trickster, as he is not being executed, but rather seeing the world from his upside-down position, where he is suspended from his ankle by a rope.

The Tarot, then, especially in the major arcana, seems to have much to say to the writer, in terms of archetype, progress through archetypes and symbolic versions of ourselves, or of our characters, to meditate on or to gain inspiration from. The cards are more generally connected to telling the future, but perhaps doing so by paying closer attention to what is present, which might be a definition of the art of reading our fortunes. Writers, perhaps more than most, depend on a sense of the future, where their art provides insight and the ability to live better attuned to the world.

Some people draw the line at divination, but it is easy to forget how much we depend on the future, how much of our lives is an investment in what is to come. So, in a sense, we all participate in predicting it, and perhaps writers do this more than most, in their unravellings and discerning of patterns of human strength and weakness. But if there are patterns in time, we can see correspondences between these and something randomly sampled, if the unconscious mind is allowed to relax into offering up connections, just in the way that creativity itself works. We also attend to chance more than we imagine, of course. 'Health and safety' are all about the 'unlikely event', but we are bound to look which way the wind is blowing.

The Tarot seems to go back to the fourteenth century, but cards used for predicting, or betting or playing games were common before that. The word 'tarot' means 'trumps' or 'triumphs' and there is a connection to trickery, to betting on the future and to competitiveness here. The Tarot was mentioned in 1781 as being Egyptian, but this seems to be false. The connection to normal playing cards can be seen in the four suits, which are as follows: Cups (Hearts), associated with water, summer, feeling; Pentacles (Diamonds), associated with earth, winter and childhood; Wands (Clubs), associated with fire, spring and youth; and Swords (Spades), associated with air, autumn and old age. The seasons, elements and ages of life are useful connections for writers.

The major arcana, which are our main concern here, have a correspondence to the first twenty-two letters of the Hebrew alphabet and also with a series of paintings of stages of initiation, so it is said. The nine Muses were once also part of its pattern, along with Apollo in cards 11–20. There is also some connection with memory training. What we seem to have is a set and sequence of emerging archetypal images, refined by a kind of folk process of what is useful and memorable remaining. A.E. Waite suggests that the major arcana were a separate game at one time. All of the cards can be positive or negative, as the cards are shuffled for fortune telling by way up, as well as order. Thus the card can be 'reversed'.

Another thing that the Tarot has in common with writing is that both address change and the balance between the static and the changing. Fortune tellers often read the cards using a 'spread' which can indicate, at the simplest level, for example, one card for the present situation, one for immediate influences and a third for goal or future fate.

For writers, being introduced to the cards for the first time, I use a simple way of getting students to respond to the major arcana. I extract the cards for 'Death' and 'The Devil', to avoid nervousness, even though these can be positive, and do not use the reversal idea. Each writer chooses a card from the rest of the major arcana, which is a plain, medieval image in the pack I favour, with only the name and number of the card attached. They then note down what they can see and what comes to them from the image.

Later, we will look at brief versions of the images' meanings, according to the material which comes with the cards, which is the Richard Gardner pack (Rigel Press, 1974), based on a fifteenth-century model. No one meaning, like anything mythic or archetypal, is definitive, however. The writers then try to create something from the discussion of their card, their notes and Gardner's definitions, either something narrative or a projection of the self into the future. Another way to begin here might be to create a story which starts with the image, as if planning a novel, like Fowles' *The Magus*.

What I do not tell the writers usually is that often they pick a card which seems to say much about their personality to me, as if I am reading them. Reading the cards as a writer can become a useful resource for seeing both yourself and others more clearly, by tuning into clues the archetypes offer.

Sallie Nichols' guide *Jung and the Tarot* (1980) offers a brilliant run-through of these major arcana images, with much literary connection. For my writers, I find it helpful to talk about the earlier two excluded images to illustrate how they might be useful.

'Death', as skeleton with scythe, is a familiar image still, which is sometimes folkloricly referred to as 'the great leveller'. It can be a positive image of the end of something as a new beginning. The scythe is a tool for a reaper, so that the image contains new life and sustaining as part of its ambiguity. It can mean transformation, therefore, and a reminder of the eternal nature of natural life, as in the ancient idea of the skull kept as a reminder of death, so as to call you to live fully. Sallie Nichols quotes Yeats' poem 'Death' and underworld journeys are here a parallel. The narrative is a place to pass through and be tested, as with Dante in *The Divine Comedy* or the heroes of the great epic poems, where this encounter with the dead brings new purpose for the future. Read as a writer, the card can take you beyond its apparent end. Death makes us humble and able to become new.

So familiar, yet still beyond us, the grim humour of the image has a liveliness which carries us forward and helps us see beyond. The writing of an elegy might be easier with the reflection on an image which many know without knowing and where you feel permission to go deep.

Card 15 is 'The Devil', which can often mean a block, or ignorance and fear and is also a symbol of human triviality and materialism. With The Hanged Man and The Ruined Tower, it is one of three 'apocalyptic' cards, where an apocalypse means 'an uncovering'. The Devil is then a fallen angel, or an angel reversed, and shows worldly values rather than spiritual. It is our Shadow side, used against us. The image is rarely used directly these days, except as a joke, but what it represents is a powerful force of denial of value, which we surely see everywhere. Jacques Brel's song 'Ca Va' explores the idea that the devil rules the world.

Richard Gardner's book *The Tarot Speaks* (1971), like *Jung and the Tarot*, is a progress through the cards of the major arcana. In it he speaks in the voices of the cards, as 'the entities of the Major Arcana seemed to want to express themselves with some force', as he says in Part One. For writers, this is an interesting experiment, in that it allows a flow of thoughts and symbolic reflections to emerge. 'Who among you risks himself for life?' he asks, in the section on Death. So the sequence becomes a kind of prophetic challenge. The book has not been republished since the 1970s but deserves attention, as it encourages symbolic, meditative thought, which becomes creative.

A novelist who has used the major cards in a similar way is Italo Calvino, in his *The Castle of Crossed Destinies* (1966; trans. 1977). Characters speak through the cards, as they can no longer speak in their own voices. The sequence of the major cards, as well as their variety of archetypes can also provide a mythical or magical journey, which writers on the Tarot have more recently been keen to explore.

There are many books on the Tarot, of varying quality and scholarship, but any that appeal to you might be useful. The best way to study them is to read widely but also to spend time with the cards themselves. Again, there are many versions of the pack. My own taste is for the older images, as they provide the strangeness of distance, which seems to aid the literary mind to go deeper. *The Original Waite Rider Tarot Deck*, conceived by A.E. Waite; cards designed by Pamela Colman Smith (first published in 1910) is still available, but my favourite, *Authentic English Tarot Cards*, published by Richard Gardner in 1974, seems no longer obtainable.

Writers have used the Tarot more than is initially apparent and a young writer recommended a book to me, which is specifically aimed for this purpose and which she finds very useful, *Tarot for Writers* by Corrine Kenner (2009).

The creative example below is a creative non-fiction essay, which attempts a breakthrough to seeing things more clearly via a sequence of the major cards.

Creative Example

The Hermit's Escape from Hell

We are only too familiar with the shattering of illusions, but we are often unable to think that there is anything behind them. Visions of the current world as hell are perhaps the most persuasive of our modern myths and you can think of your own examples, old Dantes or new. Hell clouds our vision, so we only believe what we see. Some of my favourite hell-gazers are T.S. Eliot and, more recently, Bob Dylan and Elvis Costello. Costello's Tokyo Storm Warning (*Blood and Chocolate*, 1986), written with his then wife Cait O'Riordan, has lines from verse one about realising he's in hell, and the chorus says that we cannot take life seriously because of this. This seems to me to sum up the kind of empty, disgusted view of the west I am talking about. This Is Hell (*Brutal Youth*, 1993) says therefore that nothing has value. The important thing here is that hell is a state of stasis, which any student of hell will understand is the worst thing. Promised all material life, we everywhere act out symbolic death.

Surely there is a hidden myth we might find to help, if myths, as surely they once did, have a useful function. And there is much talk of this, from conspiracy theories to self-help guides, but to the hell-gazer, it can all seem part of Costello's hellish bitter laugh. In magic, there is said to be a Secret Tradition of occult words and rituals, or the notion of The True Tongue, or Lost Speech, where things are at one with their names, where being and knowing are the same. Myths are often about what we have missed: 'Some life, yet unspent, might explode/out of the old lie burning on the ground', as Dylan Thomas wrote in 'I Have Longed To Move Away', another hell-gazer's song.

Myths might seem to be in hiding over this, offering only their tendency to avoid easy answers, like Proteus. Just as myths are infinitely responsive to attention and to interpretation, they have an equal and opposite capacity for hiding. They hide in triviality, children's tales, escapism, archaism, snobbery, pedantry; in boredom at their elusiveness, allusiveness, their paradox, their clever lie; in Tricksters, hucksters, Changelings, Blind Sight and Dionysian ambiguity; in sensationalism, dogma, fascism and taboo. They invite you not to take them seriously, as a test of whether you can see below your hell-gazer's surface. They hide in our Shadows. So we are lost, but lostness could be a step towards being found.

Where should we go? The mythic route is into the wilderness, the underworld, retreat, into that 'dying to the world' we have already started. The Hermit is an archetype, a tarot card which starts a sequence I am following to find 'some way out of here', to quote another song. We step aside to get another perspective, to experience quietness. The Hermit represents a regaining of consciousness, a growing away from the cynicism of hell-gazing, a regaining of innocence. The Hermit is part monk, part academic and he makes us feel foolish, but that is good and he might say that The Fool, the unnumbered element, the moveable, is a good name for someone seeking a non-static wisdom.

The Hermit says that hiding alone is not enough and this is not what he in fact is doing, but rather lighting the way, as in the tarot image, where he carries a lamp. Symbols only work if you continually renew your relationship with them. So the message of The Hermit ends up sending us back to the world, as a separation must be a preparation for some kind of renewed engagement.

It feels a bit shocking to the newly disillusioned to engage with Fortune, who might be the glamorous seeker of success, prone to hellish highs and lows. But through the image of the next tarot card, The Wheel of Fortune, we might be reminded that there is no escape from change. Awareness of change is intended to make you lucky and Fortune works to make you in tune with change, as in the *I Ching* or *Metamorphoses*. In the static world it looks like 'Go For It', but the risk is for more than 'It'; rather, to see the cyclical movement and perhaps go *with* it.

To accept The Wheel of Fortune is to try to do, consciously, what you once were able to do unconsciously, before the world got you stuck with it in perpetual adolescence, wanting Fortune without risk. In the image of The Wheel there may be a top dog, but others are coming round. The wheel gives form to movement. The Hermit has sent you to The Fortunate Fool, who says lighten up and go with change. We have gone to one opposite and then to another, dynamic opposite.

The arrival of the creative, magical Muse-Goddess power of The Enchantress is a next step to the middle of the sequence, both of the major arcana and of our search. Her number eleven is a renewed version of the number one card. The Magician (one) is young creative energy, setting out. The Enchantress is a more sustainable version of him, being the unconsciously fertile possibility brought to consciousness. She is central, the still point amid the turning. The creative movement will always be the essence, a summation of the last two images. To enchant is also to sing things into being. It is a rebalancing of true female creative power, which is source and birth. In Italian she is called The Force, the real power in the world. Mediation and mercy are her qualities and they charm the world into harmony. In the image she overpowers a lion with ease. She has the power of imagination, of fluent life force that defeats brute force. There is a central, cumulative maturity here.

And we might stop there, except that the next card compels us on. The world is changed for us but we want to know how to live in it. Next is the most enigmatic and strange card, but having come so far, we might identify with it more strongly. The Hanged Man sounds sinister, but we feel used to that now, seeing the world upside down, just as he does, suspended by his ankle from a frame. He is more rooted, his head is closer to the ground now, but he is framed, just as The Wheel is, as a deliberate image. We have become conscious of being able to see beyond surfaces, if we choose. We might feel suspended: another name for him is Suspense. We are between worlds, between hell-gazing and a more creative vision. He represents the loss of Ego, the awareness of difference. He might be stuck, but he sees both ways.

Our hesitation at the absurdity of these images is embodied here. Thus suspended, everything seems ridiculous. The world is upside down, as we have found it, but he is also closer to the creative earth, as are we. He is humiliated but grounded and full of visions of the uncomfortable truth. He sees through the world at last. He is an image of a change of mind. He invites us into the earth, because that is where his head is at.

Glancing at the next card, Death, it seems we have to die more deeply to escape the hell we have seen through. To give up the Ego completely, as The Hanged Man says we might need to do, feels right, if we have got over the absurdity of having the world reversed, again. How many deaths are there? There was the death from innocence, into a kind of adolescent stuckness, until you learn to see creative possibility in a more conscious way, but now we feel that, instead of one extra death, there might be two. This second death is not a death-in-life, as is the first. It is rather one leading to a rebirth from being suspended between the creative and the absurd. This is the death of the rational 'adult' ego. Myths are hiding the Shadow archetype, which is communal, unconscious, but the source of all our connection to the world.

The death of myth, where we began, meant it was hiding in this rehearsed death. All the tarot cards have positive as well as negative aspects, all can be reversed and seeing death as a positive might be hard, but it seems to clear the mind, yet again. We have to understand that understanding is a process and not a fact and this is the death of clever theory. As Tom Chetwynd says in *A Dictionary of Symbols* (1982), 'the Conscious Ego ... wants to grab the content of the unconscious without giving due respect to the powers that rule there'. Sallie Nichols, in her *Jung and the Tarot* (1980), quotes Goethe above her chapter 'Death': 'So long as you do not die and rise again,/You are a stranger to the dark earth.' Death, as Costello might suggest, is the old comic skeleton with the scythe. But the scythe is an image of harvesting, where nourishment is gathered, joining his tarot image with that of Dionysus and Jesus, as a symbol of sacrificed renewal. The King must die, if it is the King of the Ego, but our inner strength must be reborn: long live the King. Mourning gives us perspective and even our vain rationality will not help us. Nicholas of Cusa, the fifteenth-century mystic says, when talking of 'Paradise ... The door whereof is guarded by the most proud spirit of Reason, and, unless he be vanquished, the way in will not lie open.' In the midst of death, we are alive.

Temperance is the next and final step, here, into moderation and also back into time, as in the meanings of the word, which has a time-honoured feel. The balance of the flow of change and exchange, makes flight, which is the imagination, possible. She is earthly, yet capable of soaring, as Temperance is depicted winged and her stance is graceful in movement. She is a liberation from rigidity and, it seems, thus an angel and an alchemist. The two vessels she pours between are said to be mixing water and wine, both nourishing essence and the celebratory, both conscious and unconscious energies. Angels appear in order to make a revelation or, significantly, to raise the dead. She is the opposite of the Devil's view of the world, with which we started, and she means that a real change is here and that life can go on.

The world, with its mesmerised hell-gazers, will again cloud our vision. The Thief of Faith is a name for this. I found this phrase in a remark by Dylan Thomas about his poem 'In Country Sleep', where 'the Thief is anything that robs you of your faith, of your reason for being'. His last poems seem concerned with trying to see through the despair of the world. 'In Country Heaven' is about nuclear annihilation and ends with the line, 'Heaven is blind and black', which seems to me a penetrating hell-gaze.

These, then, are the seven ages, the seven pillars, the seven veils which hide the secret myth. We are in this story, but we cannot believe it, so it vanishes, as it must. We see it again in the inarticulate comedy of telling, in the way of The Fool.

Write About

Chose a major arcana card and plan a novel based around that character or archetype.

Choose a major arcana card that speaks to you and speak through it.

Use the seasons, elements and ages connection of the four suits to create a description of the symbol that represents them.

Follow the choosing of a card from the major arcana, as described above, excluding, if you wish, Death and The Devil, and meditating on the image before looking up its meaning. Then create either a narrative about the image or a projection of yourself into the future via the image.

Choose a sequence of major cards and create a narrative through them, or else a piece of creative non-fiction.

Research spreads of cards for fortune telling (e.g. present; influence; future) and use them for narrative purposes to plan a piece of writing.

Magical Texts and Literary Examples

Magical

Richard Gardner. *Authentic English Tarot Cards* (1974).
Sallie Nichols. *Jung and the Tarot* (1980).
A.E. Waite. *The Pictorial Key to the Tarot* (1911).
A.E. Waite and Pamela Colman Smith. *The Original Waite Rider Tarot Deck* (1909).

Literary

Jaques Brel. 'Ca Va' (1954).
Italo Calvino. *The Castle of Crossed Destinies* (1966).
Elvis Costello. *Blood and Chocolate; Brutal Youth* (albums, 1986; 1993).
John Fowles. *The Magus* (1966; 1977).
Richard Gardner. *The Tarot Speaks* (1971).
Corrine Kenner. *Tarot for Writers* (2009).
Dylan Thomas. *Collected Poems* (1952).

8

I Ching, Oracle and Creation

The roots of the word 'oracle' are connected with oration and with the speaking of a ritual, although the first meaning of oracle in the *OED* is of a place, only the fourth being a person. The book as oracle links back to the source then and to writing as a kind of divination. We write to see where we are and to step outside our immediate vision into the mirror images of creativity and see what they can say of us, from us and to us. Examining the Tarot, it is easy for a writer to evade the question of divination in contemplation of a sequence of archetypal images. Consulting the *I Ching* involves direct interaction with this aspect of the book. The advantage of this is that the language of the *I Ching* is that of images, the drawback might be our Western unwillingness to take the chance of casting yarrow stalks, coins or tokens seriously in the first place.

One way to begin to take divination seriously is to know that the title means the great book ('ching') of changes ('I'). Understanding and adapting to change is something we all have to do and much writing is about: how to cope with change or how to make change happen. The images and balances of the six-line 'hexagrams' of the book are based on the binary yes/no of yang and yin, where a broken line is yang, indicating change, and the unbroken yin, the static. The balance, through images of nature, between the predictable and the unpredictable, is not without connection to our ways of thinking.

Accepting that the moment is significant and that small indications are present, if we could only see them, are also not unfamiliar concepts today. If all things have potential meaning and significance, though not necessarily in a causal way, as Jung asserts in his 1949 'Foreword' to the translation by Hellmut Wilhelm (1951), then we can use the oracle usefully. The danger is to take it too literally, as with all literature and especially anything magical or mythical, and the paths to folly from this are many and strong, as extremisms demonstrate. But, for writers, the connections to the great magical source of creativity, the unconscious, are there in the poetic language and imagery of the great book. 'Creation' is the first hexagram and begins the oracle in a way we would recognise. Jung himself mentions his own consultation and how it helped him.

Approaching divination as a writer means that we take creativity seriously, which also happens in the moment of connection to some sort of fluency within us. This is perhaps beyond our immediate control, at the moment of composition. The amount of work that the questioner of the book does, both in focusing a question and in brooding on the result, amounts to a correlation between the creative process and divination.

The book is generally large and intimidating at first glance, but is also full of resonant phrases and, given a few pointers, easy to use and, as many commentators say, best got to know through use, rather than merely as reading matter. As with the creative, it is not sensible to concentrate on the unfamiliarity, but to trust in the process and see where it takes you. The unconscious mind leaps to make the connections and spark the clarity writers seek.

As with writing, clarifying a question is often the first step. It is best to have something specific but not a simple yes/no. As Jung does, it might be best to think of the book like a person you respect, then formulate a question carefully, which will give them scope to pass on wisdom. Here, again, you are moving, as writers do, from the subjective towards the objective, in a process of clarification towards useful images and phrases. What you seek is a different way of seeing how things are now, which might cast a light on the future.

It is worth mentioning that we do attend to chance in the West, even if we think we do not. Some days we see connections and other days we struggle to see them. We also look, as a society, at chance in a negative way, if we think of 'Health and Safety', with its holy capitalisation. The tricks of betting attend to our superstitious human nature, but the oracle attends to this in a more positive way. Attending to the promise of the moment is a move from small detail to a bigger picture, whereas science tends towards the opposite, where rules are proved or tested. To pause and feel which way the wind blows is sensual and instinctive, as much as a measurement.

The tradition with the *I Ching* is that one can consult it personally. This is not so true of the Tarot, where to consult it is mainly considered best via an experienced reader. This again makes the book one more step closer to writing. With a writer's way of understanding, in images, resonance and associations, the answers are not nonsense.

To work with this chapter usefully, the reader might go on to use the book themselves, but, taking my cue from Jung, it has seemed inevitable that I must demonstrate use by an example. It is beyond my scope here to go into the history of the book (usually dated from about 1000 BC), although that itself might be a source of some creative ideas, but rather to show how the oracle can be attuned to our own creative practice. Information about the use of the book can then be given in context and the whole process described in action.

The most explicit use I know of the *I Ching* by a writer is the Syd Barrett song 'Chapter 24' from the first album by Pink Floyd (*The Piper at the Gates of Dawn*, 1967). The lyric repeats phrases from hexagram 24 and from the Wilhelm translation to make a mystical-feeling song. This was not uncommon at the time among groups who were reading these texts for their poetry as much as for their use and is, then, not a bad place to start.

The first stage of finding the right question is a focusing exercise, probably familiar from some advice about formulating a thesis for an essay. This is of course also useful for any writing, though it might not take place at the stage of planning. The revising of 'creative' work is often where these decisions are made. My attitude has always been that anything that helps improve work is worth doing. So a focus on the central theme before and after, when it might have changed, is no bad thing.

The next step in any writer's work is a question many of us will ask. But how to get this expressed well enough to use presented a problem. An either/or question is too difficult to interpret, so the need to be specific arises. From formal to informal writing, to subject direction, I wavered until I came to the question of narrative. I have always thought narrative of great importance, but in my own work on songs and poems, do not always find it easy. In the end I decided that this question was specific enough, but also left scope for wider thoughts: Should my writing be more narrative based?

In posing this, I wonder if I am avoiding bigger questions or even more personal questions about my life which might need answers, but remember that the book has a way of telling you these things, if needed. To ask about writing seems a sensible thing to ask a book, somehow.

I decided to use the Wilhelm edition, called *The I Ching or Book of Changes*, translated into English by Carey F. Baynes (1951; 3rd edition 1968), which I bought way back in 1974 and so have used before, though I have three other editions, two more recent.

In most versions of the book, two methods are given for finding the six lines which make up a hexagram. One is the use of traditional fifty yarrow stalks, but this is fairly complicated, so it is usually replaced by the use of coins. Using three coins, you choose one side, say heads, to be yin and the other to be yang. Yin will count as 2 and yang as 3. You toss the coins and add up the 2s and 3s, to make 6, 7, 8 or 9. The number 6 is a broken line with an 'x' in the break; 7 is an unbroken line; 8 a broken line; 9 an unbroken line with an 'o' across its middle. These are old yin; young yang; young yin; old yang. The lines with indications in the middle are the lines that change the hexagram into another one, for further consideration. You begin the lines from the bottom and find each one of the six in order from there. This is all easier than it sounds here, by the way.

Recently I have been using another method of casting the lines. This method uses an unequal number of tokens but is more mathematically aligned to the yarrow method than the coins method is, so I am told. You need one coloured token for the 6 line; five of a different colour for the 7 line; seven of a different colour for the 8; and three different again for the 9. I use buttons bought from a local seamstress.

I will write down the question and then select six tokens and write down the resulting lines. My buttons are in a small box and I shake them up and take and return one button at a time, writing down the lines as I go, then looking up, with the key of lower and upper trigrams at the back of the book. You need care and concentration for all this, which is a kind of ritual that, interestingly, suspends time while you go through the process, unthinking. This is useful for your mind to relax before reading the results.

The hexagram I got was number 56 (of 64), which is the traveller, the stranger or the wanderer. The latter term immediately made me think two thoughts. First that the writer is metaphorically a traveller and one whose mind wanders, so that the oracle was answering me in my own terms. Secondly it made me think of the Anglo-Saxon poem called 'The Wanderer' from the *Exeter Book*. The writer, then, has all the problems and needs of the one who travels, while staying at home. The book emphasises the need for modesty and a strong moral sense sustaining the traveller, so as to survive and avoid the dangers of being like an 'internal émigré'. This idea and phrase come from the writings of Raymond Williams. The wanderer is full of strong ideas, the book seems to say, but must present them modestly and with good sense.

The Legge translation says, 'If the stranger or traveller be firm and correct ... there will be good fortune.' And 'The traveller in a resting place ... not at ease in [his] mind.'

Looking up 'The Wanderer', it is the ending which surprised me, not having read it for some time. There is a modest wisdom and a view of some kind of peace. The wanderer contains worlds of unshared experience, like a writer, but does not give in to despair. So my question seems answered in a brilliant way. Writers are exiles in the real world and must wander in the dark places of creativity, but carrying that story, which must be what writers write, is a delicate balance between internal strength (the mountain) and stillness, with the fire above it, which is creativity, which does not stay. This is not a task for everyone, as settledness is only an inner option. The dilemma of the artist is that of the exile. The narrative is lived inside and truths hard-won.

My writing task here might be then to try to write a version of the old poem, but that would be a big undertaking. Taking part of it as a metaphor for writing might be a good exercise (see 'Creative Example' below). The following poem is a sketch of some of these thoughts. It is worth noting that lines which are indicated as transforming (or old, in some terms), the 6 or 9, will turn into another hexagram, which indicates a further development.

Creative Example

The Writer as Wanderer

The wanderer at home
filled with images
while stillness can carry you away
must then make a home of a wandering mind
and show everyday modesty
when the world sees the road in your eyes
and in your stay-at-home message of restlessness

Let change be slow
and your new worlds be cautious
to make small earth
for strangeness and distance are in your words
and you must make them useful

This note-like poem sums up some preliminary thoughts about writing being narrative in nature and the writer being a narrative being. Using the *I Ching* yourself is the only way to see if you can find its riches. I have certainly found much to suggest subtle reflection in its use.

Write About

Create a question to ask an oracle, related to your writing.

Look up how to use the *I Ching* via coins, then use an online version to ask a question about your writing. Be open to suggestion and see what happens.

In a group of writers: choose six persons to choose a number between 6 and 9, then write down and look up the resultant hexagrams. Discuss the meanings and associations of the results, then all write something based on the images and insights.

Find a literary parallel to a consultation of the *I Ching* and write in response to the oracle and the other source (as with the above: hexagram 56 and 'The Wanderer' Anglo-Saxon poem).

Magical Texts and Literary Examples

Magical

I Ching, translated by James Legge (available online; 1899).
I Ching, translated by Wilhelm (1951; 1968).
I Ching, translated by Ritsema and Karcher (1994).
I Ching, translated by Ritsema and Sabbadini (2005).

Online versions are also available to consult, of varying quality.

Literary

Pink Floyd. 'Chapter 24'. From *The Piper at the Gates of Dawn* (album, 1967).
'The Wanderer' (Anglo Saxon poem), available online and in Kevin Crossley-
   Holland. *The Battle of Maldon and other Old English Poems* (1965).

9

The Magic Nine, or How to Use the Muse

As we have seen, magic often offers us ways to begin writing. One of the oldest ideas about inspiration is that, rather than coming from within, it comes from without. The Muses, simply put, are Goddesses of inspiration, who go back at least as far as the Greeks. They personify and embody the otherness of inspiration, the feeling of being in flow, as we might say now, or being taken over by the writing. The persistence of this tuning into some unconscious or unknown source persists in the reported experience of writing, so much so that it is almost commonplace.

Writers have invoked the Muse somehow and the writers of epic used to do this directly, at the beginning of their works, from Homer on. A twentieth-century writer, like the poet W.H. Auden, talked of the Muse, but mainly avoided beginning a poem by a direct invocation, as although the idea was still around, it was a rare writer who addressed it directly. So while most contemporary views of the Muse do not dismiss the idea, the received wisdom is that the Muse is most likely to visit someone who is already working. This is sensible advice. As Auden says in 'Writing', from his essay collection *The Dyer's Hand* (1963), the Muse 'appreciates chivalry and good manners, but she despises those who will not stand up to her'.

Looking at the Muse, as well as their multiple and several different individual natures can, though, bring benefits of inspiration to writers now. Finding a way to address and summon inspiration is always going to be useful.

The reason writers do not do it now is partly for the simple reason that you do not want to sound stupid or pretentious. Using an old, mythic, slow and stately beginning is going to turn the reader off, the thinking goes, and exclude people who are not familiar with the knowledge you have. For the earliest writers though, the Muse was a device of humility, not one of self-aggrandisement. In calling on the Goddesses, you were insisting that you were not greater than them and that you would be a messenger for something bigger than yourself. Beginnings of writing continue to set out the writer's intention. Perhaps the opposite of invoking a Muse might be the rappers' 'bigging-up' of themselves as a way of starting.

The Muses seem to be old Goddesses, even for the Greeks. According to Hesiod in his *Theogony*, the Muses are related to the race of the previous, more primitive giants called the Titans. They are fertility Goddesses at one level, associated with flowing water, another image of inspiration and they have a primal energy that gives us the idea that they might be linked to Diana, the nature and Moon Goddess, who might kill any passing man, like Actaeon, who does not offer her proper respect. Nature might offer us a way into being able to call on the Muses directly.

The original Muses were said in one version to be three in number: Aoide, who means Voice; Melete, who means Performance; Mneme, who means Memory. To the original, pre-writing poets and storytellers, memory was hugely important. With books and the internet, we might think we do not need memory as a writer now. But the habit of having and developing a good memory is still an essential tool for the writer. The accretion of subtle and detailed insight and the ability to retain that are, arguably, what make a writer good.

You also need to write memorably, to create phrases and images that sing in the mind. It has become a noticeable trend recently that performance poets will often recite from memory, to enhance their performances, with the sense of freedom that gives to the writer and how impressive it looks to the audience. Singers learn their songs. If something is worth singing, it is worth learning by heart. Writers who perform are now doing the same. In the age where everything is available, so they say, on the internet, the impressive old-school skill of performing your own work from memory is making a comeback.

Composing by memory was something that A.E. Housman used to do when creating his poems. He composed while walking, running through the lines and adding as he went along, in a kind of walking meditation invocation. This made his lines full of memory and memorability. The oral nature of our culture, which still persists despite the commercial appropriation of it by social media, means that we still need to talk to each other face-to-face. People's conversation is full of the charged energy of memory and one of the main faults of creative writing can be the tendency to sound too formal, too artificially like literature.

So it is possible that musing on the Muses might lead us to be less rather than more formal. If we want our speech to be inspired, we also need a bigger dimension, so a focus on an otherness can also help us not to be too inward-looking. Thus memory and Muses can give us both immediacy, memorable writing and a wider, outside perspective. The Muses tune into the otherness of writing, which is its magic.

The Muses have the strength to give us the truth, then, to animate our writing with inspiration and make it re-membered, or to put it all together in a living, true form. Another reason to invoke a Muse might be to find truth despite the writer's own limited vision. Yet can the Muses also tell us lies? Auden thinks so. Again in 'Writing', he says that the Muse can be, to writers, one who 'takes a cruel delight in telling them nonsense and lies, which the poor little things obediently write down as "inspired" truth'. Even so, he does believe that when writing it is 'as if there were two people involved, his conscious self and a Muse'. Negotiating with the Muse for true inspiration is not only a theme of inspiration, but also a subject in itself of a literary work.

'Thomas the Rhymer', a traditional ballad poem collected in the border areas between England and Scotland, depicts an encounter with the Queen of Elfland, whose sole purpose in taking him with her to an underworld of inspiration seems to be to give him a way to the truth (see also Chapter 4). 'True Thomas lay on Huntley bank' is the first line of the ballad. He is commended to tell truth always, at the end of the story, even though he is uneasy about this, by being given 'a tongue that can never lie'. Again, there is honesty, rather than artificiality, about being in contact with, or acknowledging, the source of inspiration. The Goddess, or Goddesses, correspond with an inner, unconscious level of deep truth.

There are no fixed versions of myth, especially of the traditions of the Muses, which seem to be the archetypes of inspiration. The nine Goddesses named by Hesiod have gathered about them folkloric aspects and specialisms which mean you can choose a particular Goddess for your subject or genre. Thus you belong to a line of writers going back before Christ and gather a tradition of strength and energy, however modern, post-modern or free from such 'isms' you might be. The truest, humblest writer is part of this secret tradition of the inspired.

For my own purposes, I created a list of the nine Muses, plus the 'original' three, making twelve in all. With the older three, I also listed three aspects of each of the Nine, making a total of thirty items. For my own classes and personal use, I made thirty cards of these, so that a writer could pick a subject and a Muse to work with, by choosing one card from the shuffled pack. Other ways to use the cards are to choose one to represent a character, a second one to represent or suggest a starting point and a third to be a point of crisis. A different way was to choose a first card for a character, then a second for an inner, or deeper aspect to that character. You could make and use these cards yourself or create your own version of them. Below is a list of the details I included on each card:

1. Aoide. Older Muse. The Singing Voice. Subject: voice.
2. Melete. Older Muse. To Learn; To Perform. Subject: performance.
3. Meme. Older Muse. To Remember. Subject: memory.
4. Clio. Glory, Proclaimer, wears crown of laurel, carries book and plectrum. Subject: history.
5. Clio, as above. Subject: romance.
6. Clio, as above. Subject: playing a song.
7. Erato. Eros, love, playing lyre, roses and myrtle. Subject: sex.
8. Erato, as above. Subject: love.
9. Erato, as above. Subject: tenderness.
10. Melpomene. Songstress, carries crown and dagger; tragic mask. Subject: tragedy.
11. Melpomene, as above. Subject: sadness.
12. Melpomene, as above. Subject: doom.
13. Euterpe. Beauty, pleasure; wears crown of flowers, plays twin pipes. Subject: pleasure.
14. Euterpe, as above. Subject: beauty.
15. Euterpe, as above. Subject: flowing song.
16. Thalia. Comedy; carries comic mask and shepherd's crook. Subject: comedy.

17. Thalia, as above. Subject: nature.
18. Thalia, as above. Subject: tending animals.
19. Polymnia. Many songs, hymns; dressed in white with finger to mouth in thought. Subject: hymn of praise.
20. Polymnia, as above. Subject: deep thinking.
21. Polymnia, as above. Subject: public speech.
22. Terpsichore. Whirling dancer; plays flute; invented dancing. Subject: song and dance.
23. Terpsichore, as above. Subject: whirling.
24. Terpsichore, as above. Subject: the chorus.
25. Urania. From the sky; mountain queen; carries globe; blue robe with stars. Subject: cosmic.
26. Urania, as above. Subject: night sky.
27. Urania, as above. Subject: space.
28. Calliope. Beautiful face, eyes and voice. Carries scroll and writing tablet. Subject: epic.
29. Calliope, as above. Subject: hero.
30. Calliope, as above. Subject: writing.

There are many other ways of thinking about the Muses and using their power. Their order is also given differently. Hesiod lists the Nine thus: Clio, Euterpe, Melpomene, Thalia, Erato, Terpsichore, Polymnia, Urania, Calliope. In the order I favour, I imagined a progress through the subjects they represent, which I include as an example of the multiple ways of musing on their harmonious call to be inspired.

A Writing Progress Through The Muses

Much is said about 'finding a voice' in discussion of learning to write. But it might be true that the *desire* to sing, or to write something true, means that the voice will find *you*. One of the first three Muses, **AIODE**, the Muse of voice, will give you the voice you already have, if meaning and being in tune with what needs saying is there with you.

When the voice is ready, the performer must prepare. Whether your rehearsal is for actual performance, or for writing better (writing is a performance in itself), or more useful work, your success is based on practice. Being a writer is being someone who rehearses their craft, who performs their craft, who is happening, expressing the meaning of the Muse of performance, **MELETE**.

To write well, to sing and be a practising writer, you need to command your mind, which re-members, puts back together, the shape of meaning from experience. The writer's job is to remember the truth we forgot to retain, to keep the Muse of memory, **MNEME**, alive.

Thus the glory of the proclaiming of the truth of experience, of the past in mythic context, will play through you, in the name of the Muse of history, romance and singing the song out, **CLIO**.

Love will animate your work, as it is always sought for by the reader, who seeks a kindred spirit through the words. Your love will be a youthful, erotic song and the Muse of love, **ERATO**, will take your sympathy out into the world.

History will show you glory and love, but also the darker things of life, the tragic, through the Muse of tragedy, **MELPOMENE**.

However, death and doom remind us of how beautiful the world is and how our job is to flourish in it, so **EUTERPE**, the Muse of fluent beauty can act like the scent of flowers in your words, as they flow.

Fluency is the flowing of life through you, and the great art of true comedy, where the world is turned upside down for new meaning and for happiness, can come tumbling in tragedy's and beauty's wake. The Muse of comedy, **THALIA**, will lead you back to the primal festival of growth and rural life, when the mad world is challenged.

Hymns of praise are a communal, public song, like the end of a Shakespearean comedy, full of confidence in their art which reaches out. Writing praise is hard to do well and requires talent, experience and understanding. The Muse of the thoughtful, public sphere, of many songs, **POLYMNIA**, sings in the voices of the many.

Beyond thought, the writer approaches the divine through imitating the whirling, patterned, ecstatic dance of the profound, beyond mere intellect. The Muse of dance, **TERPSICORE**, will invent your dance.

In your dance, you will become cosmic, inasmuch as the Muse of the universe **URANIA** will show you the view from where the gods stand, the wider view, the overview, which your hard work might deserve. She creates worlds and holds the universe in her hand.

Finally, the Muse of the heroic, **CALLIOPE**, is the writer at full strength, who writes and is the hero of their own worth and work, in the epic of creation.

This reads a bit 'new age' perhaps, but it does show how working through these personifications approaches some of the mysteries of writing. Writers can use the Muse, which seems to be singular, a unity or harmony of song, as well as plural, or multiple, as in the above cards and sequence of ideas about writing.

Modern writers use the Muse in different ways and decidedly not as directly or fully as Hesiod with his 116 lines of invocation in the *Theogony*. Bob Dylan's 'Hey, Mr Tambourine Man' is a song invoking a muse who sings for him. Eric Clapton's 'Layla' is a hymn to a Muse-like figure from an Arabic story of unrequited love, where an unattainable loved one often becomes the Muse for a writer. This is following in the tradition of Petrarch, who invented the sonnet about the unattainable love of a woman. The idea of the Muse involves an acknowledgement of the strangeness and fascination of the opposite to oneself, one's other half, unknowable, yet commanding and representing our desire to communicate, to go beyond ourselves.

Modern philosophers might call the Muse 'the other' and a Muse can also be a mentor figure, the person we learn from and try to please in our writing.

A writer who talked much of Muses was the poet and classicist Robert Graves (1895–1985). His book *The White Goddess* is devoted to the subject (see Chapter 4) and he did ask various women to be his Muse in real life. This raises the question of the gender of writers. As Goddesses of an older, matriarchal world, as I suggest, they are female, to show fertility and the power of creation. How a writer identifies with them is, it seems to me, up to them. A female might like a male Muse: Apollo was said to be associated with them, but the sexually ambiguous Dionysus, also a fertility God, might be a better Muse for a woman writer, or for a writer who did not want to be gendered in any conventional way. Your Muse is your own, yet part of a long tradition.

But do not get above your Muse. Know that inspiration comes through you and is not in your power alone. To think it is you only is arrogant and the old Gods and Goddesses were there to tell you this hubris is folly to humankind.

In the *Iliad*, Homer tells of Thamyris, who challenges the Muses.

> And Dorian, famed for Thamyris' disgrace,
> Superior once of all the tuneful race,
> Till, vain of mortals' empty praise, he strove
> To match the seed of cloud-compelling Jove!
> Too daring bard! whose unsuccessful pride
> The immortal Muses in their art defied.
> The avenging Muses of the light of day
> Deprived his eyes, and snatched his voice away;

> No more his heavenly voice was heard to sing,
> His hand no more awakened the silver string.
> (from Pope's *Iliad*, book 2, beginning at line 594)

Unable to sing or play, or to see, the poet is doomed and no longer alive, or connected to the immortals via the Muses, who are daughters of Zeus or Jove (Greek or Roman names for the top God). Do not worry about 'mortals' empty praise', but realise that participating in song, in the harmony of writing, is greater than you and something to do with humility and with truth.

Creative Example

The Students' Muse

> I didn't write this; it's dictated to me
> In some clear dream of fantasy
> I don't know how it sounds to you
> But to me it just rings true:
>
> If what I say on writing's clear
> A Muse is whispering in my ear
> The Muses give us education
> They tune us in to inspiration
>
> So when you write well, write to me
> For, as you now will all agree
> No teacher or student's a genius –
> It's just the Muses singing us

The magical and mythical material I am devoted to teaches me as much as I can teach anyone and that is true of this book. Muses have been depicted many times by visual artists too, and one which is a particularly inspiring image is the painting of Urania and Melpomene by French artist Louis de Boullogne (1654–1733), created around 1688. It shows Urania, the Muse of the sky, who is normally depicted carrying a globe, here carrying what could be a spherical astrolabe (star taker), so she can plot the stars from this map of the universe. Books are around both Muses, as Urania seems to hold, or create, the world, even the universe, in her hand and her dreaming eyes look heavenward. This is a picture of the magic of writing.

Write About

A friend of yours who could be a Muse, as they are an opposite of you. Or a person you do not know who has a fascination which inspires.

Think of something you think your writing lacks, find a Muse to address this and imagine them writing to you.

Write an invocation of a modern Muse, like a 'Mr Tambourine Man' or 'Layla' figure.

Write a beginning which calls on memory, as Nabokov's *Speak, Memory* does.

Imagine a Muse seeing you writing and deciding to help or hinder you.

A conversation with a Muse about lies and truth.

A parody of a beginning, calling on the Muse, such as something starting with a line like this: 'Inhabit my mouth/O Goddess … '

Start a piece of writing by asking Nature to inspire you.

Rewrite Thamyris' story in a contemporary setting.

'Come write me down, ye powers above/The man that first created love', begins a traditional folk song ('The Wedding Song'); emulate this beginning for a subject you want to write about.

Magical/Mythical Texts and Literary Examples

Magical/Mythical

Hesiod. *Theogony.*
C. Kerenyi. *The Gods of the Greeks* (1951).
Joseph Campbell. *Creative Mythology* (1968).
In Our Time. BBC Radio 4. 19 May 2016.

Literary

W.H. Auden. 'Writing', in *The Dyer's Hand* (1963).
Alexander Pope's translation of Homer's *Iliad* (1720).
Robert Graves. *The White Goddess* (1948), and poems.
Bob Dylan. 'Mr Tambourine Man' (1965).
Eric Clapton/Jim Gordon; Derek and the Dominoes. 'Layla' (1970).

10

Gurdjieff and Colin Wilson: The Woken Moment

My 1970s copy of *The Occult* by Colin Wilson (1971) has a lurid green cover, with the title in purple and the legend 'The ultimate book for those who would walk with the Gods' below, taking up a third of the space. I always feel that this ludicrous-seeming claim is of its time, but also that it indicates something of the ambitions of magic which still seemed manifest at that time. Arguably, since then, the 'Mind/Body/Spirit' section of bookselling has aimed a little lower, to a kind of hobby market, or fashion section. I still recommend Wilson's book to writers I teach, however, not only because it is a comprehensive and readable introduction to many areas of its subject, but also for the literary enthusiasm which he shows, in making the whole pursuit of the magical something which empowers the imagination. Throughout his work, this is a common thread and thrust of what he has to say.

Colin Wilson might agree that the Enlightenment was an attempt to open up the human mind by the use of science, which ended with science seeming to close it down. I would say the 1960s and 1970s revival of interest in the occult generally was a kind of post-Enlightenment project to take hold of the idea of scientistic progress in the mind and point a way forward. The interest in such matters in the nineteenth century began this and it was taken up again, after the interruptions of two world wars, when a new kind of optimism bloomed.

This optimism is there from the first line of Wilson's introduction. There is no doubt how seriously he takes it, or how ambitious for his subject he is. 'Civilisation cannot evolve further until "the occult" is taken ... at the same level as atomic energy.' This kind of optimism is rare nowadays, though not lost entirely, but the serious, almost evangelistic tone of *The Occult* is catching and has an opening effect on the mind which has lasted.

A new level of mental evolution was the aim and the possibility of living forever was dreamt of again. Like the Romantics, with their interest in 'the sublime', in the 1960s, sex and drugs and music offered moments of transcendence, which seemed to wake the individual from the sleep of post-Second World War, post-industrial conformity. All of Colin Wilson's work is in search of these moments, in search of what he often calls 'faculty x', or what one of his heroes, the psychologist Abraham Maslow, called 'peak experiences'. This was the cure for anxiety or the neurasthenia of the time.

Where do you find this kind of breakthrough? The Romantics found it in Nature and its effect on the mind:

> ... another gift,
> Of aspect more sublime; that blessed mood,
> In which the burden of the mystery,
> In which the heavy and the weary weight
> Of all this unintelligible world,
> Is lightened.

These lines from Wordsworth's 'Tintern Abbey' (1798) would still resound in the writers today who are concerned with eco-criticism, psycho-geography or new nature writing. As Wordsworth says, later in the poem, ' ... in this moment there is life and food/For future years.' Here we have the heightened 'moment' and the promise of the 'future'.

Writers have always been interested in these heightened moments, then and now seeking to live more intensely, and have sought to recreate these moments for revisiting and for their readers to share. All the highest and lowest songs are about magic moments, one way or another. James Joyce called them 'epiphanies'; William Burroughs called them *The Naked Lunch*, which was the moment you saw everything clearly for once. Epiphany is a Greek word, meaning 'manifestation', used as a Christian term for the manifestation of Jesus to the Magi, or of Christianity to the world. There is then something of the magical about it and of the revelation from a new world to an old one, a sense of breakthrough and again, of progress. Joyce uses the term in *Stephen Hero*, an early version of *Portrait of the Artist as a Young Man* (1916). It seems present in literature from many eras and present especially in the work and thinking of Colin Wilson and of one of the thinkers he explores in *The Occult*, George Ivanovitch Gurdjieff (1866?–1949).

Gurdjieff, as he is usually known, became a cult figure in the 1960s and 1970s, where some of his central ideas were reflected in books and films and by rock musicians. Kevin Ayers' song for Soft Machine, 'Why Are We Sleeping?' (1968), holds one of his central insights, which is that, because of habit and convention, most of us are as if sleeping, unless we break through into an epiphany, into our 'faculty x', or our woken moment, as I have put it. One of Gurdjieff's insights was that religions had lost their original purpose, resulting in such catastrophes as the First World War. He might yet be proved right.

The drug habits of that walking-with-the-Gods era were connected with this, along with the renewal of interest in Aldous Huxley's experiments with mescaline. The derangement of the senses to achieve breakthrough were found in the work of Rimbaud, as in the trancelike nature of the writings and music of that time, from Bob Dylan and Neil Young, linking them with some of the dance music of the present day. Gurdjieff was interested in dance as a way of breaking through.

Dylan and Young both talked of learning to do consciously what they had previously done unconsciously or via smoking cannabis, in the case of Young. These moments of inspiration, however achieved, are then essential to writers. Are they unconscious, or a kind of superconsciousness, as Colin Wilson suggests, or another version of the Muses (see Chapter 9). Writers seek inspiration but, crucially, they seek to pass inspiration on to their readers.

According to Gurdjieff, older, symbolic forms of consciousness, sometimes called primitive, sometimes called advanced, were the original purposes of religion. We have become automatons, in the fears and desires of our zombies and vampires and need to suddenly STOP!

Gurdjieff did this with his dancers, to make them break into an act of self-remembering.

Colin Wilson talks about the novel *The Haunted Woman* by David Lindsay (1922), in which someone is haunted by a possible life of clearer vision, of woken-ness, which is occasionally experienced in another, usually unseen, part of a house which she has gone to look at, with a view to buying. Later, she and the man selling the house go there together and see it as a place where their lives could be fulfilled or 'realised'. They try to remember how to get there, how to conquer the forgetting that happens in the 'normal' world. Wilson says this is an image of Gurdjieff's ideas.

After I read this myself, I experienced a dream in which a past relationship manifested itself as present in an extra basement part of the flat where we had lived in the past. This, in turn, had reminded me of a time when much younger, when I had been reading Freud at night, about dreams sometimes being about 'wish fulfilment', and I had dreamed of myself and my first girlfriend building a shack in a green field. Finding somewhere to live together was difficult then, as now: we were both living with our parents. These dreams had something in common, that great sense of possibility which Gurdjieff's teachings seemed to offer and which Colin Wilson seeks to convey in his writing.

While Gurdjieff is perhaps better read via his disciples, Wilson is above all a writer. His own novel *The Philosopher's Stone* (1969) describes a scientific experiment in which a particle of metal is introduced into the brain, which has the miraculous effect of a gradual widening of vision and awareness.

Both these novels have been hard to get in the past, as if the rare woken moment were hard to find in fiction as well as fact, but are now available easily again. However, a first edition of Lindsay's novel would cost you, at the time of writing, at least £1,500 and Wilson's novel at least £400 (about $2,250 and $600).

Books that deal with the progressive, mind-opening aspects of the occult are often themselves about books and their rarity, as are perhaps all books about magic. A more recent manifestation of this is present in the popular novel *The Celestine Prophecy* by James Redfield (1994), where the search for a revelatory 'Manuscript', always presented with a capital 'M', is sought, which describes the next stage in human evolution as a new kind of religious awakening. Some recent books that address an alternative sense of progress will be discussed in the Postscript, where magic and the future are explored.

Whether this optimism about the future is accurate, or just another dream of progress as the popular myth of our scientific and materialistic age, is an interesting one to explore. Whatever we think of it, however, there is no doubt that the heightened state, in all its various manifestations, is sought and disseminated by writers. Their method of composition is also their subject, as we have often discovered here, just as it is their purpose for the wider world of the reader. The defamiliarisation idea of Russian critical literary theorist Shklovsky somehow connects with the near-contemporary Russian Gurdjieff, in the idea of using language that wakes up the reader.

There is no doubt that the journey into the self and the seeking for correspondences in the world are part of the echo-sounding a writer must undertake in order to make their writing a series of versions of the woken moment.

Creative Example

The Iron Stairs

Only a moment leaves you yearning –
When you feel the whole world turning
And stillness is a point of vision
When you've shared a sacred mission.
Can Love or Nature recreate
When all the senses integrate
Within the flow but not the flood
And blessings of the world come good?

On the top deck of the bus
Our moment wasn't obvious:
We joked and talked and saw anew
A rare but common conjoined view –
Can well-trod iron stairs relate
How much that they can elevate?

The poem seeks to emphasise the gap between ordinary life and the woken moment, which might sometimes seem in human communication much narrower, and yet still feel out of reach. An ordinary, shared, top-deck bus journey becomes a shared revelation. The gap between the technology of the titular stairs and the pathetic-fallacy-like, archaic, over-poetic asking them to speak also rehearses these gaps between the real or ordinary world and the woken moment.

Write About

A moment in your life when everything seemed strange, but clear. And describe a method for recreating it.

Lost love in terms of epiphany, using language which 'makes the world strange', as in the literary concept of 'defamiliarisation'.

Imagine a 1960s character on the verge of a breakthrough via an interest in the occult, trying to explain it to sceptical friends.

An interruption which makes you suddenly see the reality behind things.

A disillusioned writer of progressive magic writes an apology.

'At the still point of the turning world' is the poem which begins section II of 'Burnt Norton' from T.S. Eliot's *Four Quartets* (1944). Write about a dance or movement which creates a new and non-moving head space in a participant.

Research Gurdjieff's life and find a moment which illustrates his ideas to write about, or one that interestingly contradicts or challenges them.

Magical Texts and Literary Examples

Magical

P.D. Ouspensky. *The Fourth Way: In Search of the Miraculous* (1957, 1949)
Colin Wilson. *The Occult* (1971).

Literary

Kevin Ayres. 'Why Are We Sleeping?' (1969).
T.S. Eliot. 'Burnt Norton' (1944).
David Lindsay. *The Haunted Woman* (1922).
Colin Wilson. *The Philosopher's Stone* (1969).
William Wordsworth. 'Lines; composed a few miles above Tintern Abbey, on revisiting the banks of the Wye during a tour, July 13, 1798'.

11

Yeats' Apparatus

W.B. Yeats (1865–1939) had everything at once, as a poet, and his reputation as the best poet of his time has continued, with no one seeming to come near him. He resonates in the public, private, prophetic, traditional and contemporary spheres simultaneously. He is tantalising to other writers because he seems at once accessible and serious, as if he should be a good model for future writers and yet somehow remains alone on a great height. The closer you get to him the more baffling he becomes. For us writers then, what was the equipment that made him write as he did and is there a way we could use the same methods? Like Shakespeare, he is at once ours entirely and yet beyond us. He is, also like Shakespeare, admired as much as read. Some of this is to do with magic.

The magic side of Yeats, about which he was unambiguously vocal and definite, is often dismissed, even by critics who rate him as the best poet of our time. Here, the bafflement goes the other way. We insist on the poetry but in every word he said about it, he was at pains to stress how magic was at the heart of everything he did. Readers of this book might have an understanding of magic as being at the centre of creative writing, so might then have a better chance of going along with him and gaining some clear view of the elements of his craft, both in his worldly and other worldly methods. What did he bring with him when he went to write?

One place to start is to notice that, as a student of Blake, as a student of the Tarot and as someone whose own magical system was based on contraries and opposites, these places where reversals and paradoxes abound are echoed in his writing. He is full of opposites to us too: personal, yet political; radical, yet conventional in poetic form; easy to read, yet difficult; populist, yet a user of mythic and philosophic traditions; attached to place, yet universal in his appeal. If we can get to grips with these surface ambiguities, we might get closer to understanding the magic sweep of his appeal.

It is even possible that his lack of respectability, in relation to his insistence on magic and therefore his methods of writing, has been like a magical protection or even enhancement to his reputation. His reputation as a poet has never wavered, unlike say Philip Larkin, but his disreputable connections to, for example, automatic writing, have preserved his mystique as beyond us, to say nothing of his political and Irish situations. These are ambiguous too, of course.

Looking carefully at his work and his life, as well as his literary context, we can begin to see him as deserving of admiration for his whole, intimidating self, as a writer who is useful rather than baffling and unapproachable as a model.

One clear place to start is his childhood, where the magical element enters his life early. The folkloric and the attachment to place are aspects of the traditional in his work. Another ambiguity is the balance of tradition and being a very contemporary writer, but it is worth looking at the idea of tradition as being a way of being present in the world, of the use of what is passed to us, which is what tradition means. Writers are traditional in the way they use what they have around them in the best way. So again, it is what apparently might have made Yeats nostalgic or passé that somehow manages to help make him contemporary.

Much has been written about the female influences on Yeats, but biographers only mention in passing the intriguing figure of his uncle George Pollesfen's servant, who has the wonderful name of Mary Battle. She sounds to me like a Yeatsian contrary, as her name means 'peace' and 'war', as in Mary as Mother of God. She was a woman with second sight, who would set a table with an extra place in the foreknowledge of someone unexpected by others turning up. It was not just that this woman existed, but that Yeats came from a family where this was taken seriously, as the uncle was, like Yeats, part of the Golden Dawn magical group and a practitioner of astrology. These older things were fashionable at the time when he was a young man, but for Yeats they were not a dabbling, but part of something of direct use to him in his writer's equipment.

Biographers of Yeats will emphasise his youthful influences, from his mother's family, which rooted him in a kind of pagan Ireland, but as if that was somehow separate from the public poet. However, it does provide, I would say, a connection between that and his public, political world. The supernatural for Yeats was a connective, rather than a disconnective, thing. Further connections are to be made in the history of Irish popular poetry and song. A poet like Thomas Davis, who Yeats directly mentions in his work, had already established a public, national voice. Again, Yeats was part of a connective tradition.

What is remarkable about Yeats and his magical apparatus is how ahead of his time he was in making these links between the public and the private life. The fact that he came from a family where art was the norm and was thereby a second-generation bohemian must have made him more open to taking a broader, more serious view of his craft. His message to writers who come after him is then in part the need to be absolutely serious about integrating your art and your life.

A writer who has a good view of Yeats in historical context is Dudley Young, in his study of the poetry, *Out of Ireland* (1975). Rather than brushing aside the magical in Yeats, Young starts with it and sees sympathetic magic as a kind which writers use to praise or damn the things they write about. The breadth of a poet can then be seen as particularly relevant to Yeats, as 'by giving us access to the past and the future, the poet can offer us some hope of access to the present'. So from here in his introduction, Young makes Yeats as a poet of magic the only clear way to see his primary qualities. The progress of the mechanical world, the loss of religion and the rise of the individual all led Yeats towards magic as a way of reconnecting to the serious world via poetry.

When young, Yeats was part of the end-of-the-century decadent social and artistic world, so was already an outsider to the conventional. His movement between England and Ireland, his being from Protestant Anglo-Irish stock already made him someone in a place to question identities. Dudley Young says:

In any case, by 1914 the main outlines of his poetic enterprise had emerged. The possibility of being a bard for all Ireland had gone, indeed had never really existed, and he was an isolated Anglo-Irish Protestant with aristocratic ideals in a country that was to be dominated by the Catholic petty bourgeoisie. What gave his poetry such a wide metaphoric range was that his Irish situation was analogous to that of western Europe, about to shatter its traditional culture in the Great War. When cataclysm comes, everyone takes to the road with his tent. In certain respects Yeats joined the exodus; but as poet-mage he tried to stay behind, to haunt the shells of the burnt-out houses. He resolved to summon and propitiate the departed ghosts in the hope that he might find a home amongst them ...

Thus Young places Yeats as a resister against the tides of destruction via his historic, poetic and magical apparatus which might usefully confront the madness of his times. We tend to think of Yeats as the ultimate insider of Ireland, but it was the opposite of that which made him, made him serious, and even makes the rest of us writers identify with him in his effort to make the world better. In one of his most popular poems 'When You Are Old', the praise he offers to the youth of the one addressed is to the serious and questing side of them. As Young suggests, magic was part of this, not, as some critics have said, an escape from the public, serious side.

Yeats was then always the outsider inside, a position from which to question and to work hard on what needed to be said. As Young points out, again from his introduction, the magician in the West, like the poet, is an isolated figure. Yeats then had his marginal place and ambiguity preserved which was part of his art, part even of his protection against grandeur or triviality. Some of his late poems emphasise the need to have foolishness as well as passion, and indeed contraries, as part of his store of balanced images which might be reversed.

From his historical perspective and his folkloric, maternal family, combined with his open-minded bohemian times and paternal family, Yeats was ahead of his time in seeking a unifying symbolic and mythic view or apparatus to help mend the world. If we look at his statements on writing and his writings on magic, with this basis to start from, we can begin to make sense of him as a whole writer and see his influence as not one to follow without understanding its integration.

Yeats' principal work on writing is *A Vision*. Before Robert Graves' *The White Goddess* (1948; 1961) and Joseph Campbell's *The Hero with a*

Thousand Faces (1949), *A Vision* (1925; 1937) has a similar intent, which is to create a unifying, symbolic language for poetry. However baffling some of his writings, outside the most popular poems, can seem, the intention is both magical and serious.

Trying to read *A Vision* is not a good place to start to take Yeats' magic seriously, although A. Norman Jeffries' introduction might be. He says that Yeats was always, from schooldays, interested in Odic energy, or the power of Od, but also aware of the way it seemed to others. His great heroine Maud Gonne thought the Golden Dawn a lot of stuffy middle-class Brits, for example. He did try to link his magic to his Irish roots by forming his own society but also felt that the poet sought a different thing from magical interests, namely the cyclical rather than the fixed and the images rather than some kind of unity.

The shifting cycles of personality and of history are thus at the heart of *A Vision*. Reading the book itself, though, we come across the fact that it was a collaboration with his wife, and derived from what is called automatic writing. This stops many readers dead in their tracks. Messages which are claimed to come from elsewhere seem a hard thing to take seriously.

If you know about Yeats' writing methods, however, you might begin to see what energies automatic writing might have offered. Yeats, despite the lyrical qualities of his best poems, was not, surprisingly, an 'inspired' writer when it came to putting words on a page. It seemed the poems did not usually come to him fully formed, but by great effort. *Yeats at Work* (1965; 1978) by Curtis B. Bradford describes his manuscript pages as bafflingly complex and massively worked on.

People imagine poets working, and many poets do work, from lyrical impulses and fragments of vibrantly poetic lines towards a full-formed poem. Yeats, however, would begin a poem by writing a kind of prose summary, which many might do as an end or editing part of the process. He might then decide on form and rhymes before endless drafting and redrafting of lines, gradually making the poem less abstract and more lyrical. Knowing this, almost a reversal of what conventionally is seen as poetic technique, we might begin to see how Yeats needed magic to connect his hard work to the lyricism he wished to achieve. In a way, it might be said his technique was like that of his artist brother and father, where the beauty of the picture only emerges at the end of the process, or where detail is built up into the whole. His process also resembles a magical ritual, a gradual summoning up of poetic power.

He also worked hard to make his work personal, or dramatically characterful we might say and modern in speech. These were decisions he made, rather than impulses he followed. Again, in this way he managed to be both worldly in hard work and magical in intent. He recognised how he needed the magic to balance and interpret not only the world outside but also his own working methods. The fact that his wife, Georgie Hyde Lees, who married Yeats in 1917, was able to provide him with messages from magical sources must have been just such a balancing of the inspired which he needed.

Looking at the 'Table of the Faculties' from *A Vision*, someone familiar with the Tarot might not feel so baffled. This looks like a practical system of shifting archetypes, which might be used straightaway by a reader. If we go along with Yeats, we can find his magical connections have come to fruition here as apparatus and will guide us towards his own accessibility, which was never in doubt, even if how he gets there might have been. The task to explain and make useful the insights of *A Vision* seem to me still to be there to do, despite even a new website (yeatsvision.com) attempting this to some extent. The fact remains that some of his greatest poems were written using his system, such as 'The Second Coming' and 'Leda and the Swan', to take two examples.

Taking *A Vision* as crucial can make understanding what Yeats has said about his own work easier to follow, as can the wider magical context we have already looked at. In 'A General Introduction to my Work' (1937) he is at pains to distance himself from the personal in poetry. Like T.S. Eliot, his great contemporary, he seeks something more universal than the cult of individualism of his day. This can again be baffling to a reader, as Yeats seems the most straightforwardly personal of many poets. Understanding his magical concerns and writing methods, we can see that he seeks to speak in a personal way but not in the narrow concern of self-expression. His directness is achieved by the alchemy of his creation of a dramatic and symbolic representation of a voice. The result may feel direct, but his attachment to tradition, to symbolic and cyclic resonance and to a kind of dramatic mask means the personal becomes universal and that these contraries are deliberate and in balance.

In *Yeats at Work*, at the end of chapter one, the author records Yeats moved to tears by some bad poetry of homecoming, but realising that the truth of the direct speech was something not to be thrown away, despite his more public announcements against self-expression. The magical, which is about universal forces as well as about the unconscious, can be seen as linking the powers to the voice. Yeats' knowledge of the universality of the mythic and folkloric then give him a directness which becomes more modern than modernism. More than Eliot or Pound, the other great poets of his day, who helped him modernise, he integrates by his closeness to magic, his modern-ness into his accessibility, which only makes us appreciate him more. Yeats' disconnection from the ordinary was a way of becoming more relevant to the ordinary world and this is what makes him, paradoxically but deliberately, the most political of poets.

His sense of place was that of a wanderer at home, his resistance of his separation made him integrated and his use of contraries and the impersonal make him the most personal and direct of poets. Like William Blake's *Songs of Innocence and of Experience*, he achieved simplicity through a balancing with its opposite in a kind of magical transformation towards the purity and power of speech, made into lasting songs.

Yeats is difficult to be influenced by well, as his art has a deeper root, or route – a deeper magic. Like any great writer his surface looks easy and there are writers who try to imitate his style in a superficial way. It seems to me that we are still only just getting towards understanding his magic, his apparatus, all of which has protected him from us and yet made him still relevant to us.

Write About

Look at Yeats' 'Table of the Four Faculties' from *A Vision* and write something exploring a particular phase and the contrary energies described there.

Create a piece of writing using a reversed method to the one you usually employ and even write about something you do not normally address as a subject.

Yeats' poems are full of much-quoted phrases, often used for titles. Find a phrase which appeals to you and has not been used by others (best check via the internet) and write, trying to see the contraries and paradoxes in the subject.

Do you see yourself as an insider or outsider? Write about how you can be usefully both.

Do you have magical stories from your childhood or family? How might they be useful now?

Try automatic writing by getting yourself into a calm state and writing down a question and allowing your unconscious mind to wander. Let the writing flow without thinking directly. Alternatively, find a book on the practice and follow the instructions.

Attempt to write something very lyrical and personal by first using planning and impersonal methods, as if planning an essay on a science topic, or developing a character for a drama.

Research a magical aspect of Yeats' life and write about it (as in the 'Creative Example' below).

Creative Example

To Mary Battle (Yeats' uncle's second-sighted maid)

Of all the women who used their power;
    Now gone or hiding, flesh or air,
    There's one could see what isn't there
In her most ordinary hour;
    Who set a place for one unknown,
    Who, unexpected, then would come.

Her first name peace, her second, war;
    Her natural gift of second sight;
    Who held her contraries so light

That you might sense what they are for;
    An uncle's maid set at your feet
    What all your strivings might complete.

A kinder magic, less than grand,
Sets a place for a poet's hand.

Magical Texts and Literary Examples

Magical

A. Norman Jeffares. *A Vision and Related Writings* (1925; 1937).
Edain McCoy. *How to Do Automatic Writing* (1997).
Website: yeatsvision.com

Literary

Curtis B. Bradford. *Yeats at Work* (1965; 1978).
R.F. Foster. *W.B. Yeats: A Life* (Vols 1 and 2; 1998; 2004)
Louise Morgan. 'W.B. Yeats' in *Writers at Work* (1931).
W.B. Yeats. *Collected Poems* (1994).
Dudley Young. *Out of Ireland* (1975).

12

Shakespeare's Magical England

If W.B. Yeats is a difficult magical writer to ignore or to be influenced by usefully, then Shakespeare is impossible. But even saying that might give us a starting point, as part of Shakespeare's magic is just that – doing the impossible. Shakespeare is like God, as people even doubt his existence, as well as his identity. He is also an unapproachable old monument which looks like no help to writers, unless you want them to feel useless, or hopelessly up to date. My feeling is that we do not celebrate him enough in England and are too reverential and referential and tend to leave him to the literary experts. Yet, like Yeats, it may be that if we approached him as a local magician and with a sense of wonder and fun, we might get closer to him and find him on our side. The one thing that is worth emphasising is that he was a popular writer and a performer himself. His saving grace is that he was closer to the ordinary world, with all its fertile and rude magic, than it might seem.

Some of those productions in modern dress in 'experimental' theatre are closer to him, in principle, than dry study, or making kids too young to understand him read his stuff. But the first thing to notice is how much magic there is in his work. If you look in your 'Big Book of the Unexplained' type of volume, you will not find Shakespeare listed and even scholarly editions of his most magical play *The Tempest* do not much discuss magic, in their apparatus of notes, introductions and sources. Why is this? The tendency of magic to be occult, to protect its presence, is not to be underestimated, but if approached correctly, we can find it easily. Also, Shakespeare does so much else so well. There is a Shakespeare for everyone and this is part of his magic. Magic is also part of his magic.

Again, like God, we tend to project our needs onto him, which is good for the critical industry, but less so for writers. If we start to think of his impossibility as a kind of magic in both the writing and the subject of many of his works, we might then make Shakespeare more magical, more English and more useful. It might be possible that projecting more of our magical selves is a key to him.

Ted Hughes has been the main writer to address the magical aspect of Shakespeare's work. The mixed reception and the negative criticism he got for his *Shakespeare and the Goddess of Complete Being* (1992; 1995) was perhaps only to be expected. Hughes' introduction covers why and is useful to us here. It has to be admitted that Hughes' book is a bit of a monument and has its forbidding aspects, but is essentially, as Marina Warner said, 'enthralling' and liberating.

Again, as with Yeats, writers will excuse my crude summing-up. Hughes suggests in his book that Shakespeare, like Yeats, evolved a mythic structure for his writing, like a plan, a key or a dominant myth, which he used with variations. I see a connection here with Robert Graves' mythic, poetic pattern, as outlined in *The White Goddess* (see Chapter 4), one of Hughes' favourite books. Both myths are connected to a Goddess and both to the cycle of her suitor who is killed and reborn anew in a cyclic pattern, with variations. There are many versions of this myth but there seems to be a strong link to the imagination in its search for a greater truth. These myths are of love and death and are religious myths as well as ones which animate creativity. Hughes locates Shakespeare's inspiration in his long poems *Venus and Adonis* and *Lucrece*.

Hughes' main point is that Shakespeare had a magical structure of images, inspired by the magical thinking of his day, which made him the great writer he is. Human life in a male–female polarity of death and rebirth is connected to all of Shakespeare's subsequent work via the two poems. The great interest in magic of Shakespeare's time is best personified in the person of John Dee. Dee was a scientist/magician and, as Hughes reveals, described himself in a text as Shakespeare's 'master'. Dee was also influenced by Giordano Bruno, as were many at the time. Some of these magical thinkers wanted to free the world from the narrow views of Catholic and Protestant into something more liberated. They influenced many later thinkers who sought to rescue Christianity from its narrowness.

As mentioned above, they were also scientists and Hughes says that this is why Shakespeare's realism and insight into character, for example, is praised, even though it is influenced by magical ideas. Later considered discredited, this magical influence stayed with the poets and playwrights. It is worth mentioning that theatre, so attractive to Yeats and T.S. Eliot, two other magic writers, is a ritual place where the magic of words comes to life. Shakespeare not only used these things but discussed them often within his plays. On pages 32–33 of Hughes' book, he gives an outline of the benefits of his system of thought. Having a system of images is helpful to a writer and he suggests that a means of ameliorating the spiritual conflicts of his day was appealing, in the way it might lead to a better, more integrated world, via the creative imagination of spiritual love. The process of images, archetypes and cycles was also useful, as was the idea of theatre as a microcosmic version of the system. The last two points he makes emphasise the ritual and magic elements of theatre, where these things come to life.

When you begin to look at Shakespeare as a magician, seeking to heal the ills of his time, things begin to make sense. Hughes is at pains to say that Shakespeare is a mythic writer, but one who can connect his magic to his realism very well, via his use of his mythic/scientific understanding, in a prefiguration of psychology. The occult tends to have its occult protection built in, as if Shakespeare designed his work to appeal to the real by his own 'so potent art', as Prospero says. Yet when you look at the magic in Shakespeare's work and how often he discusses it, it becomes astonishing that it is so little discussed. Jonathan Bate's fine book about Shakespeare, *Soul of the Age* (2008), has no entry for magic in the index, for example.

Most writers who use a mythic system as a source seem to become obsessed by a particular myth, which they find fruitful to return to often. Edwin Muir's two poems about horses, one written at the end of his poetic career, one at the beginning, come to mind, as the magical dimension is much present in both. Hughes' myth seems particularly aligned with Shakespeare's in the subject of love, when he mentions the work of Sylvia Plath and when you remember that his *Birthday Letters* (1998) were to be published within a few years of his Shakespeare book, to great acclaim.

Anxiety about revealing the magical is there in Hughes' introduction and rightly so. This seems to me to echo the anxiety of Prospero, the magician in *The Tempest*, where it is an anxiety about how these ideas will be received, even about magic itself having both the tendency to be the creative energy behind serious work and also about people's inability to see it. This is the strength and dilemma of the artist and the artist's magic.

One of the most famous instances of magic and its discussion in Shakespeare's work is via the ghost of Hamlet's father:

> **HORATIO**
> O day and night, but this is wondrous strange!
>
> **HAMLET**
> And therefore as a stranger give it welcome.
> There are more things in heaven and earth, Horatio,
> Than are dreamt of in your philosophy. But come;
> Here, as before, never, so help you mercy,
> How strange or odd soe'er I bear myself,
> As I perchance hereafter shall think meet
> To put an antic disposition on,
> That you, at such times seeing me, never shall,
> With arms encumber'd thus, or this headshake,
> Or by pronouncing of some doubtful phrase,
> As 'Well, well, we know,' or 'We could, and if we would,'
> Or 'If we list to speak,' or 'There be, and if they might,'
> Or such ambiguous giving out, to note
> That you know aught of me: this do swear,
> So grace and mercy at your most need help you.
>
> **GHOST**
> [Beneath] Swear.
> *They swear*
>
> **HAMLET**
> Rest, rest, perturbed spirit!
>
> (*Hamlet*, I. v)

Hamlet is saying I might have to seem crazy for anyone to believe it and that strangeness is part of the wider picture. Reminiscent of Hughes' book and of the condition of magic and its discussion, the famous quotation sums it up well: 'There are more things in heaven and earth ... than are dreamt of in your philosophy.' Hamlet begs his companions to go along with him, as Hughes does, as, miles more humbly, even I do in this book.

The greatest attack on magic is another famous passage, sometimes read as positive, which is another example of the occult nature of the occult:

HIPPOLYTA
'Tis strange my Theseus, that these lovers speak of.

THESEUS
More strange than true: I never may believe
These antique fables, nor these fairy toys.
Lovers and madmen have such seething brains,
Such shaping fantasies, that apprehend
More than cool reason ever comprehends.
The lunatic, the lover and the poet
Are of imagination all compact:
One sees more devils than vast hell can hold,
That is, the madman: the lover, all as frantic,
Sees Helen's beauty in a brow of Egypt:
The poet's eye, in fine frenzy rolling,
Doth glance from heaven to earth, from earth to heaven;
And as imagination bodies forth
The forms of things unknown, the poet's pen
Turns them to shapes and gives to airy nothing
A local habitation and a name.
Such tricks hath strong imagination,
That if it would but apprehend some joy,
It comprehends some bringer of that joy;
Or in the night, imagining some fear,
How easy is a bush supposed a bear!

HIPPOLYTA
But all the story of the night told over,
And all their minds transfigured so together,
More witnesseth than fancy's images
And grows to something of great constancy;
But, howsoever, strange and admirable.

THESEUS
Here come the lovers, full of joy and mirth.

(*A Midsummer Night's Dream*, IV. i)

Notice the word 'strange' emphasised again. Theseus almost praises the imagination by the end, but also accuses the poet of egomania too, but the real magician here is his wife. This five-line speech of hers answers his doubts so fully and fairly, saying, as it does that 'the story' creates 'something of great constancy'. Here we have the anxiety and the answer of the magic poet and the hope for a world more 'full of joy' by the balance, as seen in the formerly wild queen and her sensible husband, in the myth and the magic. We are 'transfigured so together' by Shakespeare's serious whimsy.

It is only magic, but do not worry, Hippolyta, 'Queen of the Amazons', says, which is repeated by Puck at the end of the play. Here 'mended', 'mends' and 'amends', said twice, is like a chorus or ritual invocation – a spell of mending:

PUCK
If we shadows have offended,
Think but this, and all is mended,
That you have but slumber'd here
While these visions did appear.
And this weak and idle theme,
No more yielding but a dream,
Gentles, do not reprehend:
If you pardon, we will mend:
And, as I am an honest Puck,
If we have unearned luck
Now to 'scape the serpent's tongue,
We will make amends ere long;
Else the Puck a liar call;

So, good night unto you all.
Give me your hands, if we be friends,
And Robin shall restore amends.

Shakespeare, in the conventional way, asks for applause, 'give me your hands', as he excuses and endorses magic, keeping the occult nature of the business in its 'weak and idle', but potent disrepute (see Chapter 1).

The play where magic is central is *The Tempest*, which rarely moves from these themes and contains, from the beginning, the anxiety with magic. It also seems most concerned with the way the world is ruled and the role of magic in this, which is why I think that the wood of *A Midsummer Night's Dream* is the Forest of Arden, not a wood near Athens and that the island of *The Tempest* is England. More of this later, but we will notice in the play how Prospero is concerned that his daughter is paying proper attention, which is part of Shakespeare's description of the anxious, resigning magician. In Act I, Scene ii Miranda is anxious about harm coming from the storm and Prospero reassures her, 'No more amazement … ', where 'amazement' also means a kind of worrying, and 'No harm … '. The questioning and the reassurance are there from the beginning:

FERDINAND
Where should this music be? i' the air or the earth?
It sounds no more: and sure, it waits upon
Some god o' the island. Sitting on a bank,
Weeping again the king my father's wreck,
This music crept by me upon the waters,
Allaying both their fury and my passion
With its sweet air: thence I have follow'd it,
Or it hath drawn me rather. But 'tis gone.
No, it begins again.

ARIEL *sings*
Full fathom five thy father lies;
Of his bones are coral made;
Those are pearls that were his eyes:
Nothing of him that doth fade

But doth suffer a sea-change
Into something rich and strange.
Sea-nymphs hourly ring his knell
Burthen Ding-dong
Hark! now I hear them, – Ding-dong, bell.

FERDINAND
The ditty does remember my drown'd father.
This is no mortal business, nor no sound
That the earth owes. I hear it now above me.

(*The Tempest*, I. ii)

The strangeness is followed by some reassurance of a link with the previous generation and remembrance of connection. The theme of the sea is present from the opening scene. An island of generations connected with the sea and the sea's natural change is surely as much metaphorically England as anywhere else. Projecting into a nowhere to tell truths about here and now is a familiar trope in science fiction. It is also worth noting that that ultimate no place/good place *Utopia* was already in existence and Sir Thomas More spelt it out, with an ironic twist, in the last words of the book, 'I needs confess and grant that many things be in the Utopian weal-public which in our cities I may rather wish for than hope for.' The words 'our cities' show that he was using elsewhere to think of home. The sea is a big hint, I think, and the cosmic sea shanty sung by Ariel.

Caliban's hymn to his island is another famous section of hope and home amid the strangeness:

CALIBAN
Be not afeard; the isle is full of noises,
Sounds and sweet airs, that give delight and hurt not.
Sometimes a thousand twangling instruments
Will hum about mine ears, and sometime voices
That, if I then had waked after long sleep,
Will make me sleep again: and then, in dreaming,
The clouds methought would open and show riches

Ready to drop upon me that, when I waked,
I cried to dream again.

(*The Tempest*, III. ii)

There may even be irony here about rain in the open theatre of the day, but the dreamy island might also not be so strange. The reference to the resigning speech of Prospero to the 'globe' is Shakespeare's microcosm, his world and his actual theatre, called 'The Globe', where England is the world and the world is the imagination. The ironic bringing it all home is there and obvious again:

PROSPERO
You do look, my son, in a moved sort,
As if you were dismay'd: be cheerful, sir.
Our revels now are ended. These our actors,
As I foretold you, were all spirits and
Are melted into air, into thin air:
And, like the baseless fabric of this vision,
The cloud-capp'd towers, the gorgeous palaces,
The solemn temples, the great globe itself,
Ye all which it inherit, shall dissolve
And, like this insubstantial pageant faded,
Leave not a rack behind. We are such stuff
As dreams are made on, and our little life
Is rounded with a sleep. Sir, I am vex'd;
Bear with my weakness; my, brain is troubled:
Be not disturb'd with my infirmity:
If you be pleased, retire into my cell
And there repose: a turn or two I'll walk,
To still my beating mind.

FERDINAND MIRANDA
We wish your peace.
Exeunt

(*The Tempest*, IV. i)

The lines which describe 'The cloud-capp'd towers, the gorgeous palaces,/ The solemn temples, the great globe itself,/Ye all which it inherit, shall dissolve' could easily be about London, especially to a London audience.

The presence of books in the play make us see the world of the writer, as does the anxiety about those paying attention to him. In Act I, Scene ii he asks, 'Thou attends not?', before being reassured, not for the last time, by his daughter. In Act II, Scene ii Trinculo says of Caliban, 'Were I in England now, as once I was, and had this fish painted, not a holiday fool there would give a piece of silver.' He means if he had this being on show in a fair, he wouldn't do much good. Imagine 'as I once was' said with an exaggerated wink! Again we have the irony of hope and mockery, as he is, when he says it, in very England, calling the audience 'holiday fool[s]'. The drinking and the 'kiss the book' swearing by the bottle, rather than the Bible, all sound like the present England too and the present audience.

'How beauteous mankind is', says Miranda, like a hope, not without irony to the audience, of the future, in Act V, Scene i, while Prospero acknowledges the native Caliban as 'This thing of darkness/I acknowledge mine'. Very near the end, the lines 'And thence retire me to my Milan where/Every third thought shall be my grave' seems to have a missing ghost rhyme, as if to read, 'And thence retire me to my Milan/Where every third thought shall be Caliban', as if loving his dark native self, his old England of magic, transformation and allegory. Whatever else Shakespeare was, he is always writing about England, with his multiple-layered cosmic Globe.

It may be that the occult has hidden this obvious allegory among the post-colonial readings that are so popular still, but a magic reading makes this play looks like a last attempt to love and make peace of all the unruly world at home, in irony, in a 'sea change' and in the microcosmic Globe of vision. Seeing Shakespeare as a writer of magic here seems to bring him more down to earth in his prophetic satire, his projection of England as elsewhere.

The poet Coleridge said it well in a lecture on *The Tempest*: 'If Shakespeare be the wonder of the ignorant, he is, and ought to be, much more the wonder of the learned; not only from profundity of thought, but from his astonishing and intuitive knowledge ... he is rather to be looked upon as a prophet than as a poet.'

There are always 'more things' to be 'dreamt of' for writers.

Creative Example

Prospero's England

I am Prospero
I let the world go

A migrant soul like you
and England too

As all come to shipwreck
Can the world's pain be cured in magic?

England my home and my enemy –
I seek to leave the world sane and sanely

Write About

Everyone in *The Tempest* wants to rule the island. Write about what kind of world you would like, as a satire of the here and now.

Poet Philip Terry's *Shakespeare's Sonnets* begin with his version of Sonnet 1. Shakespeare writes, 'From fairest creatures we desire increase'. Philip Terry's version begins, 'Clone Kylie'. Find a piece of Shakespeare you like and try to make something as daring, funny and contemporary from it.

Ted Hughes says that many writers have a myth which obsesses them and inspires them. Read Shakespeare's favourite book, Ovid's *Metamorphosis*, and find a myth that gets under your skin. Then devise a pattern from it and use it to write.

Research the witch Sycorax, referred to in *The Tempest*, and write 'Sympathy for Sycorax'.

The joke about Shakespeare is that he is full of quotations and titles. Find an unused line in Shakespeare that says something about your past life and use it as a title to write about a ghost of your former self.

Rewrite *The Tempest* as a Middle Eastern migrant narrative.

Write a new song for a magical scene in a play.

Shakespeare's original manuscripts would have been copied and then thrown away as 'foul papers'. Imagine discovering some of these. Are they fakes? Thought fake but real?

Magical Texts and Literary Example

Magical

Samuel Taylor Coleridge. 'Lecture XI', in *The Lectures 1811–1812* (Signet edition of *The Tempest*).
Ted Hughes. *Shakespeare and the Goddess of Complete Being* (1992; 1995).
Shakespeare (Arden or Signet editions of plays are especially good).
The Tempest.

Literary
Jonathan Bate. *Soul of the Age* (2008).
Shakespeare.
Sir Thomas More. *Utopia* (1516).
Philip Terry. *Shakespeare's Sonnets* (2010).

13

Faust: You Are the Lucky Fist

The story of Faust is the story of our materialistic times, about the man who sells his soul to the devil. It has everything: evil, magic, ambition, greed, lust, punishment. If it can be a pot-boiler, it is our pot it is boiling. There are versions of it everywhere and although it is not the first story of temptation, it is one of the most tempting. We have avoided evil up to now but here black magic must make its entrance. The first thing any book on magic will tell you is that the bad you wish on others will come back to you threefold. Faust is a morality tale, of course. But we get to share in the disillusionment, the lust, the power, the cheapness of self-righteous shame, thinking he is not us. But he is.

Whatever else it is, the Faust story is about writing, about books and their secret power. Faust is a disillusioned student, dreaming in the night. Writers are Faust because they too wish for words to come to life, for their outlandish ponderings to become reality. The blues singer Robert Johnson was said to have sold his soul to be such a brilliant blues guitarist and singer. He was Faust and so are you.

The roots of the story reveal something striking: Faust was a real person. Andre Dabenzies, in his essay about the whole myth, from *Companion to Literary Myths, Heroes and Archetypes*, edited by Pierre Brunel (1992), says he lived in Europe between 1480 and 1540 and that his first name was Johann or Georg. He was a wandering conman, a fake mage but one who had a degree. He was hated in his day and died horribly, his throat cut by the devil. A document from 1580 mentions his pact with the devil, for which he got power but paid with a bad death. Other stories about him say he became a legend in a combination of two people. One was a printer, giving us more literary connections, the other an academic turned magician, but that makes him even more like us and like us writers. He is real but of ambiguous identity, like us.

In 1587 an anonymous pamphlet was published in Germany, called *History of Dr Johann Faust*, which told the first written version of the story. This folkloric, dirty scandal-sheet is cheap but full of potent magic and was very popular in its time. Usually referred to as *The Faust-Book*, it can be easily found online and is worth a read. All the basic story is there, including the sex with the devil in the guise of a female, which seems usually to be the first wish. The twenty-four-years element of the pact is there, echoing a day's hours, as is the signing of the pact in one's own blood, which is another image of the writer trying to make it alive. Mephistopheles, the devil's agent and Faust's tempter, is there also and perhaps we are him as well.

Shakespeare's contemporary, and a kind of punk Shakespeare, Christopher Marlowe, created the first literary version in his play *Doctor Faustus*, first performed in 1594. Marlowe says in his Prologue that he is talking about an ordinary person, not a king or lord, but someone 'swol'n with cunning, of a self-conceit' and that 'Nothing so sweet as magic is to him', and another writerish thing: 'this the man that in his study sits'.

Act I gives us the cynic academic, sitting there dismissing all subjects, except:

> The metaphysics of magicians
> And necromantic books are heavenly;
> Lines, circles, schemes, letters and characters;
> Ay, these are those that Faustus most desires,
> O what a world of profit and delight,
> Of power, of honour, and omnipotence
> Is promis'd to the studious artisan!
>
> (*Doctor Faustus* I. i. 49–55)

This could be an advert for becoming a writer! Worth noting, though, is how shocking this would have been, how sweetly scandalous, where someone openly mocks religion in favour of magic. Marlowe was himself accused of this blasphemy in his lifetime, when it was a serious offence. The magic writer, with their 'Lines, circles, schemes, letters and characters', could be in danger. Thus *Doctor Faustus* is somehow the opposite of *The Tempest*, as all is rent rather than mended, in the end, as at the beginning.

Faustus feels that he can become a Demi-god and summons what seems to be his magic tutors, Valdes and Cornelius. The bad versus the good angel's visits come in here, where the good urges him against literature, 'O Faustus, lay that damn book aside'. Meanwhile the bad angel urges him to go forward and seeks to 'Resolve me of all ambiguities'. It is the absolute abandon to evil which makes it so attractive. The writer and philosopher George Bataille wrote about this in his book *Literature and Evil* (1957; English trans. 1985), where he says we are drawn to decay and corruption, to darkness and death and that this is a strong part of all literature. We seek to lose our human ambiguity and be at one with the world as animals are. The fastest route to this is in our yearning for evil.

There is a desperation and despair in evil too. At the end of Scene i, Faustus says he does not care if he dies. Scene ii has him summoning devils and the appearance of the manipulative Mephistopheles. Faustus asks him, 'How comes it then that you are out of hell?', to which he gets the famous and brilliant reply, 'Why, this is hell, nor am I out of it.' The pact comes shortly after this admission of dark despair, where Faustus 'surrenders up to him his soul' and will be rewarded by evil 'Letting him live in all voluptuousness'.

Not far from evil, not far from 'all voluptuousness' is absurdity, which reminds me of the comedian Billy Connolly saying that sadomasochism would not suit him as he would find it too funny. Neither the original author of the 'Faust Book' nor any subsequent writers have avoided this, and Marlowe plays it up well.

Act II sees the signing of the pact with his own blood, another classic element of the tale. The blood will not run to write, but Faust uses fire to make it, while the images of writing expand again. The contract is read aloud. First wish, first lust, arrives promptly: 'Let me have a wife ... for I am wanton and lascivious.' Then four books are required: a book of spells for power, a book of spells to raise spirits, one of astrology for prediction and one of plants. There is so much for a writer here, I feel, that suggestions for creative work, for exercises, could come unbidden from reading the first part of Marlowe's play.

The middle of the story presents a problem for all writers, from the original tale to Marlowe and all subsequent versions. The middle section of the story, one of instant gratification and worldly desire, is a trial for the imagination. It is a cliché that people do not know what they want and when they get it, it is unsatisfactory. We run out of imagination and run into absurdity. Marlowe does the disillusion well, where Faustus says 'I'll burn my books', when Mephistopheles comes to claim his soul. The famous meeting with Helen of Troy, the most beautiful woman in history, has him starting this much-quoted section:

> Was this the face that launch'd a thousand ships,
> And burnt the topless towers of Ilium?
> Sweet Helen, make me immortal with a kiss:
> Her lips suck forth my soul, see where it flies.
> Come, Helen, come, give me my soul again.
> Here I will dwell, for heaven is in these lips,
> And all is dross that is not Helena.
>
> (*Doctor Faustus*, V. ii, 99–105)

He seeks redemption through love, which is where Goethe, the next most famous writer of the tale, attempted to mend the problem of the middle.

Marlowe's end is clear, however, as his play is a tragedy. The story goes that real devils appeared onstage on the first night, so the play has its superstitions, much as Shakespeare's *Macbeth* does. But whatever else it is, Marlowe's play is a fantastic sourcebook for writers, who can get the uneasy feeling that Marlowe himself feels the analogy with writing, which we share when reading him. Our evil desires are one big fantasy in all the dangerous freedoms of writing.

Johann Wolfgang von Goethe (1749–1832), the great German Romantic poet, paradoxically got his folk version of the story first, indirectly, from Marlowe. Street and puppet theatre versions were popular in Germany in his childhood and took their story from travelling theatre performances of Marlowe's play. Goethe was obsessed with the story all his life and worked on parts one and two over most of his writing career. Goethe also shared with Faust a sickness of study and an interest in magic as a young student. His part one of *Faust* is a play that is not often performed, but much discussed. This is another indication of the problem with the play, that is, the problem of evil, which is decadent in the sense of being a dead end.

Perhaps echoing Dante in hell, the love element of the Romantics takes over the middle section and offers, in the figure of the female, some kind of possible redemption. The figure of Gretchen in *Faust* makes the middle of the story at least stronger. The folkloric and earthy energy of the tale was ever-present in Goethe's dramatic poem and he, like Marlowe, makes much of the beginning. It is worth noting that his own early version, sometimes called the *Urfaust*, itself became a legend.

Faust Part One has a slow start, where all the energy of the tale lies. There is a 'Dedication' about lost youth, giving us a clue to the overall strength of the tale and its hold on us. This is followed by a discussion between the writer, the director and a clown, which again emphasises the self-conscious writer-ness of the tale. The clown illustrates the childishness of writers and showmen in his last words in the scene: 'Age does not make men childish, as folks tell us/It only finds them children to the end' (Sir Theodore Martin's translation, 1865). Is this the moral of this primal tale of evil?

Faust seems to invite the energetic, as, if evil has one virtue, it is that of having energy, and Goethe deliberately echoes his sources in pantomime-like rough verse, called, in German, 'Knuttelvers'. Goethe's third beginning is set in heaven, so less blasphemous than Marlowe. God sends Mephistopheles, apparently, to help Faust, but the ambiguities are set up still. He summons the spirit at last but in a way the whole seems here as elsewhere like a lesson, or a satire, and as much, in the Romantic manner, about disillusion and despair as about evil.

The second main scene finds Faust in a totally opposite world of a village festival, but unable to be as unselfconscious as the ordinary people he admires. To gain the world he says goodbye to it and the ambiguities of evil are made real by this scene. Goethe begins, over again, with wonderful verse about this, often translated. Faust himself is more ambiguous, when we see, for example, that it is Mephistopheles who suggests the pact, not Faust himself, as in Marlowe.

Scenes with Gretchen as innocence and Martha as experience add to the vitality of Goethe's tale, as does the scene in the witches' kitchen and the orgy of Walpurgis Night. At the end of part one, Gretchen is saved and Faust himself survives for the late publication of Goethe's part two. Part two has 'quantitative easing', if you need a literary precedent for that. Goethe's version then reads often like a writer's autobiography, from the first dedication and 'play about making a play' elements.

Writers stuck, cursed, with beginnings are all Fausts. The word Faust means both 'fist' in German, but also 'lucky' in Latin, or favoured. So the lucky aggression of the story echoes the lucky aggression of the writer, as does the trouble with middles and ends, let alone starts that seem to bring out megalomania. The psychology of Faust then gives us some analogues to the tale and also some insights into us, as lucky fists of writers.

The oldest story of creation is one of 'original sin', which is the idea that we are creatures who cannot help sinning, as it is the price we pay for our self-consciousness. The Faust tale seems to imply the opposite, where sinning becomes intentional, perhaps in an unconscious desire to return to a kind of animal innocence. There, intention causes its opposite. But trying to be like the Gods, trying to own all powers, is the ultimate expression, at one level, of individual, willed desire. The devil offers us the opposite of humility and the fulfilment of the ego. The magic of the energy drives evil along in a thrilling but sickening beginning.

Adam and Eve apart, the clearest biblical connection is with the story of Simon, sometimes referred to as Simon Magus, in Acts 8:9–24. 'But there was a certain man, called Simon, which beforetime in the same city, used sorcery, and bewitched the people of Samaria, giving out that himself was some great one. To whom they all gave heed, from the least to the greatest … ' He hears the apostles converting and healing and 'offered them money Saying also, give me this power … ' He is told by Peter that 'thy money perish with thee, because thou hast thought that the gift of God may be purchased … Thou hast neither part nor lot in this matter: for thy heart is not right in the sight of God.'

Other parallel stories are those of Icarus, who tries to fly on wax wings too close to the sun and the whole tale of Prometheus, the great symbol of human progress with his stolen gift of fire and his terrible punishment for tricking the Gods. He is another said to be the great symbol of our age. A novel like *Trilby* by George du Maurier (1894), gives us the character Svengali, the Mephisophelean character who has become an archetype of the exercise of control over an innocent talent, owes much to the Faustian pact.

Psychologically, we all make a pact with ourselves as we begin life and, arguably, sacrifice parts of ourselves in order to function in the world. At the extreme, this is a defence against trauma and can be psychotic. There is also an element of bipolarity in the tale, where the depressed academic finds a manic energy to release him from study into an opposite energy. The cyclic nature of the magic as tragic fall echoes the extremes of this illness.

The fruitful, fearful and promising, greedy beginnings which are the main power of the tale make Faust the archetype of adolescence and of perpetual adolescence. For this reason, perhaps, Faust is us and our time. He embodies our disillusionment with ourselves and our paradoxical sense of real magic being there, if we had the courage to seek it. Further, he is our expression of this dilemma, this modern version of the Edenic tree of knowledge of good and evil. The huge potency found by writers in the myth, allowing them to make their cries about art and its limits and possibilities, makes him our analogue, our would-be famous writer.

His origin in the folkloric makes him the rude but energetic scapegoat of our basest and loftiest and most foolish desires, as well as our luck, and bad luck. What else do we write about? You are Faust.

I am Faust too. Modern versions of the tale in novels include Bulgakov's *The Master and Margarita* (1967), from which the Rolling Stones derived 'Sympathy for the Devil', and Thomas Mann's *Doctor Faustus* (1947), where the artist at the centre is called Adrian. While writing this chapter, my car insurance company phoned to say someone had made a claim against me from the 13th of the previous month. Evil tempts and evil returns and our ends are uncertain. The end of the original 'Faust-Book' is perhaps the most convincing, where the students find his monstrous, bloody corpse and he then autobiographically haunts his own house, as he haunts us.

Creative Example

'Sweet Valdes and Cornelius'

I'd only known Maggi C about a year, I now remember, when I asked her about who had taught her magic. I didn't actually know if anyone had, but, as she was teaching me, I wondered if I was a link in a chain. She laughed and told me there were two teachers. They both lived in the same town as her, a small market town on the north Essex border, called Balestead.

'One of them was called Vale – can you believe it? V, A, L, E; not veil. But a great name for the occult. He was known as just Vale. His name was John, though. He wore a cloak, even. Ridiculous. And make-up sometimes. Bit of a goth, bit of an old rock star, who had never been one. But actually a good bloke. People thought he was evil, of course.

'The other one was Chris Corner. I met him first. He had really good books and was a writer. I borrowed some stuff from him. He lived down my street and we met in the pub. He was even a bit tweedy, like a young fogey before his time. This was in the eighties. He lived alone but there were rumours of him moving there with a much younger woman – or girl. Both of the two mages had dodgy reputations. Someone said I must be selling my soul to the devil, knowing these two.

'They vaguely knew of each other but had oddly never met. I think both of them suspected the other of being into black magic. Anyway, I took it on myself to set up a meeting for them. Neither wanted it. Wonder why I did it, but I was full of positive feelings about the hidden knowledge and didn't see any harm in light and openness. Like I am still, even now, I suppose.

'There was this lovely old library in Balestead, called the Folly Library. Full of really old books from some local landowner, centuries back. It was all that was left of him. This small, domed building is at the back of someone's house that was closed up. It was owned by the council and I was with a group of scholars who wanted it opened up. We were cleaning it out and getting builders and book conservers in to look at it. I had the key and I lured the two of them there, Vale and Corner, and then left them to it. They were sitting on two old deck chairs. I went, saying I'd be back in a couple of hours.

'Chris told me what had happened the next day. Later on I talked to Vale and he told me his version of events. They matched up, but not like they'd prepared it. Both of them saw the comic side of it, too.

'Apparently, after I left, they had sat in silence for ages, as if trying to stare each other out. Silence each other out. A silence-off. But more comfortable.'

'What are we going to talk about?' Chris said, finally.

'Good and evil, I suppose,' Vale said and they laughed.

'We've circled around each other but never felt the need to meet, but the evil that attaches itself to us – magicians? Students of magic, say. Worth wondering about.'

Vale thought for a bit, then said, 'It's silly romance mostly – projection onto us. Onto me, anyway.'

'Me too.'

'But it's something that we shouldn't ignore.'

'Evil,' Chris said, flatly. More silence.

Then he said, 'The temptation when you understand more than most and the romance they put on you. And the idea of original sin.'

'Any power can be used for evil,' Vale said. 'Humans have sin built in. It's a problem of consciousness.'

'I believe in original innocence as well as original sin.' Chris said this and Vale looked interested, which he hadn't really done before.

'People want power and they want sex. That's it mostly.' Vale sat back after saying this.

'And are inclined to vanity,' Chris added.

'You talking about me?' Vale said and they both laughed again.

'I don't think so now. Just a style thing.'

Vale said, exaggeratedly, 'O, thanks! What about you and that girl?'

'Is that my evil reputation?' Chris asked.

'Yeah. Around here.'

'We were close but she needed to grow away from me. We're still in contact. She's married and I'm her kid's godfather, for god's sake.'

'Neither of us are as evil as we might be then,' Vale said. 'Disappointing.'

Maggi told me they then talked about Electric Girls. These were young women who were investigated for giving off an electric charge, before people understood electricity. 'They both laughed when they told me about this,' she said. She suspected them of sexism as a bonding mechanism. Chris's younger woman Patty had been one – electric. She had to wear an insulating armband or her watch would go wrong, from the magnetism. She was a nurse and had a plastic nurse's watch, for the same reason.

Then they talked about Faust, she said.

'Neither of us are Faust, then,' Vale said. 'We haven't sold our souls to the devil.'

'What a relief,' Chris said.

'Who are we then? We've been tempted by Electric Girls where the electricity has been projected either way. But we're maybe too ordinary. I hate to admit it,' Vale said.

'Just students. Well, in my case. There are students in the story of Faust. Disillusioned ones. Not like Maggi,' Chris said.

Vale said, 'Isn't Faust more a teacher? In Marlowe? An academic. Neither of us is quite that, though we both teach magic to Maggi.'

'Happily outside the institution, which might drive you mad,' said Vale. 'Of course, the original Faust-Book is all about sex and farce. He has it off with a female version of the Devil. Marlowe and Goethe couldn't have that explicitly. And he gets torn apart by devils and dies.'

Chris said, 'Goethe kept him alive for part two. Here, are we Mephistopheles-es?'

'Nah. Too Grand and not the Devil's messengers.'

'Hang on a minute,' Chris said, 'there these two tutors in Marlowe's play. They are magicians who come in and then disappear, like Doctor Faustus has gone further than them.'

Vale suddenly looked scared, remembering something. 'Their names are like ours.'

They both got up and began looking at the old, leather-bound books. They found a copy of Christopher Marlowe's *Doctor Faustus*. They found the names of Valdes and Cornelius, who Faustus greets happily. Valdes wants to conjure women and be like gods, always a bad idea in mythology. Cornelius wants to use 'the words of art,' like a writer.

'Are you thinking what I'm thinking?' Vale asked.

'The story about the devil actually appearing on stage at performances? Are we conjuring something up here?'

They both look round, pretending to be spooked at nothing there.

'These two old fools, pretending to see something. That's when I came in. They both agreed that this was me, Maggi, not a female devil. They explained the reference and showed me the book. Chris said it was worth money – an early edition.

'We stood there, under the dome in that little Folly Library. And the sun came out, can you believe it? They were friends after that and, though they never mentioned it, I sometimes thought of them as Valdes and Cornelius. Or 'Sweet Valdes and Cornelius', as Marlowe calls them in *Doctor Faustus*.'

Write About

The story above deals with a playful discussion of the suspicion of evil which attaches itself to magic. Write a tale where evil is projected onto others but found to be in the projectors (as in witch-trials).

Study Marlowe or Goethe's versions and decide on a minor character (as in the 'Creative Example' story above) or opposing characters to write a dramatic monologue or dialogue around.

How would your own Faust negotiate the middle (fulfilment of desires) and end (time to pay) elements of the story?

One version of the original Faust is a printer at the time of the mechanisation of printing. Does the mass-produced book (or other media) amount to a pact with the devil?

Faust the printer writes the first anonymous Faust book, aware of the dangers of writing: create him.

Faust in a different genre, as we have seen the story as magic, farce, evil, tragedy, love and comedy. What else could you do with him?

A female Faust.

A positive view of Faust as the future.

Write dismissing all the things you have studied in favour of magic (as in Marlowe's play).

Describe staging a version of Faust where a devil appears unbidden, as in the Marlowe play legend.

Use a line from Marlowe, such as Mephistopheles' 'Why this is hell, nor am I out of it', and write from there. See also Elvis Costello's song 'This Is Hell'.

Write a contract with the devil.

Describe the four magic books you would wish for (*Doctor Faustus*, II. i).

What would you sell your soul for at this moment?

Magical Texts and Literary Examples

Magical

'The Faust-Book' (1587; available online).
'Sympathy for the Devil'. The Rolling Stones (1968).

Literary

Mikhail Bulgakov. *The Master and Margarita* (1967).
Elvis Costello. 'This Is Hell', from *Brutal Youth* (1994).
Andre Dabenzies, 'Faust', from *Companion to Literary Myths, Heroes and Archetypes*, edited by Pierre Brunel (1992).
Goethe. *Faust Part One; Faust Part Two* (1805; 1831. Any edition).
Thomas Mann. *Doctor Faustus* (1947).
Christopher Marlowe. *Doctor Faustus* (1594).

14

The Lost Fairies

Has our Faust frightened our fairies away?

One thing you can say about fairies is that they are small and often gone, but even this is not certain. Fairy tales often do not have fairies in them, in the same elusive way. The Victorians, often mocked in our desire to see fairy tales as psychological archetypes and therefore a serious matter, or for their associating fairies with children's entertainment, took them seriously too, in their particular way. Fairies, as small supernatural beings, as a symbol of something lost or overlooked, remain a potent symbol. Their disappearance is significant; their lost-ness is our own. Rose Fyleman, writer for children, expressed this well in 1918, in her poem 'The Fairies Have Never A Penny To Spend' (*Fairies and Chimneys*, 1918).

It is clear in this seemingly simple, old-fashioned poem that they are other than us, old but ever-changing and always young. Rich in a different way than us, they are like a religion, which calls on the roots of all religion. Felicia Hemans (1793–1834), who also wrote 'The Boy Stood on the Burning Deck', had earlier written, in her 'Fairy Song':

> Have you left the greenwood lane?
> Are your steps forever gone?
> Fairy King and Elfin Queen
> Come ye to the sylvan scene
> From your dim and distant shore
> Never more?

In trying to think about fairy tales as source material, recent writers have not often thought about fairies themselves. It is probably true that in modern versions of fairy tales fairies are again noticeable by their absence. It seems to me that, for a book about writing and magic, it is time we addressed this loss.

Two of my favorite books about fairies and fairy tales are small books. The first is *Fairy Music*, edited by A.E. Waite of the Golden Dawn, associated with Yeats and with the Tarot (see Chapters 11 and 7, respectively). Originally called *Elfin Music* (1888) and published with the former title in the tiny Canterbury Poets series by Walter Scott, this is an anthology of poetry about fairies. The other book is Dame Marina Warner's recent *Once Upon a Time: A Short History of Fairy Tale* (2014). Both are concerned with the literature of fairies. Both have the quality of being themselves somewhat enchanted. In tribute to these and to the poem above, here is a short poem:

Creative Example

Books About Fairies …

Books about fairies should be small
And seem to say almost nothing at all
For fairies are never so easy to see
As they live so near to invisibility

Those who claim them are mocked aloud
Yet they walk among the busiest crowd
You may not believe what I know is true
But I saw a fairy once with you

She walked beside you and kept you safe
And never asked you to believe

So, to me, it is not a matter of belief in any rational way, but the belief in possibility. The disappearance is the interesting thing, even disappearing from their own tales.

The origins of fairies are also various and hard to grasp. Waite notices the revival in his time, but also sees the interest as at once traditional in literary terms (Chaucer, Spenser, Shakespeare) and as 'the salvation of modern poetry' in his introduction. One place that fairies hide is in the whimsicality they offer, as opposed to the mythic function of providing dramatised psychology. The surface quality of the fairy tale is both a strength and a weakness. Fairies are a trap for fools but an elevation for those with vision. Therefore, then, as now, they can be a mixed blessing.

The word 'fairy' is linked to enchantment via Latin and French, but can also be associated, he says, with female magicians, as in King Arthur's mystic sister Morgue La Fay. There is a connection with the old, alternative power of the Goddess, which seems to be there still in the best modern writers on fairy matters: Angela Carter and Marina Warner. The Queen of Elfland in 'Thomas the Rhymer' is another example of the strong female fairy.

After that, the child as fairy and hence the association of childhood with fairy tale, comes along, like an image of lost innocence. This Christ-like Golden Child seems to be there, for example in *Silas Marner* (1861) by George Eliot. Waite describes the fairy child as being 'of four to five years, indescribable in her beauty, sirenian in voice and manner, clothed in a robe which sparkled with all manner of precious stones, and aerially conveyed in a superb, swan drawn chariot'; she has a Castle home in the air. This is the fairy of 'French metrical romances'.

Then we get the more familiar small persons of 'Celtic' mythology. Spenser's fairies are Promethean beings, connected to Greek mythology while Shakespeare notes the Indian connection. The link with the Greek nymphs is clear, while Chaucer links fairies with the underworld of the dead via Pluto and Persephone. Fairies are obviously shape-shifters and culture-shifters. He quotes another ballad poem 'Tamlane' or 'Tam Lin': 'Our shapes and size we can convert/To either large or small;/An old nut shell's the same to us/As is the lofty hall.' This mutability and non-material strength continues to be beguiling, especially to writers, where the fairies are alternative – to whatever you wish. They seem reactive and subject to mood and are therefore like a test or supernatural indicator of a natural balance.

The poet Herrick, Waite says, makes them both of the old religion and Christian and they seem to have both kings and queens, who are often stronger, as in Queen Mab. They have no coherent history, then, but a kind of universal otherness as our alternative selves, where fancy is alive as a defence of our propensity to overinflate ourselves. However much we try, they refuse to be connected to the real and that is their great strength.

Everything has been thrown at fairy tales and yet they survive, through trivialisation, sanitation, infantilisation, academicisation; still they remain useful to storytellers and writers of all kinds. They are nearer to us than Greek myths and there are some from where you live. Their oral origins and changeability survive in the same way that fairies themselves seem adaptive. Literary transmutations date from far back, as Alison Lurie suggests in her *Oxford Book of Modern Fairy Tales* (1993), citing George Cruickshank's version of 'Jack and the Beanstalk' from 1853, where the giant is an alcoholic. As soon as people collected them, they began rewriting them, as the tales seem to invite that and respond to any serious attention, as all magical and mythical material does. The stories appeal to highbrow and lowbrow and many are about the fulfilment of potential and the rites of passage of initiation into adult or more individuated life and the confronting of the darker things in life.

The archetypes of female power are there in the tales, as is the 'Jack' figure, who is the younger, questing male, the weaker man who becomes strong. Robert Bly famously made a whole book about male maturation from one Grimm tale, *Iron John*.

The idea of the fairies being lost is always present. They have been seen as a link between humans and angels, and also as having had their own world once and now being nomads. They are light, or even made of light, and they are our ultimate personification of some subtlety we seek or have lost. We all have our own, domestic versions and interpretations of them. The great collectors sought them for national identity but also found a universal language in them. They are often giving messages about how to survive and how to go on towards a happy ending.

Katherine Briggs, in her *Dictionary of Fairies* (1976), suggests, in her entry 'Departure of the Fairies', that this was always the case in literature. She quotes from Richard Corbet (1582–1635), in his 'Farewell to the Fairies' (published 1647). This begins 'Farewell rewards and fairies', which refers to fairies being given to children as sources of gifts for good deeds, as in the 'tooth-fairy'. This gift for being good as a natural thing still remains folkloricly today. The poem was also the title source of Rudyard Kipling's book *Rewards and Fairies* (1910). In the poem the fairies were 'changelings' who brought merriment to labour. 'Witness those rings and roundelays/Of theirs, which yet remain', he says, noticing the connection with nature in the fairy ring growth of fungus with dancing and circles. He mentions their suppression by authority but their ability to transcend religion, despite being of 'the old profession'. The last stanza talks of keeping secrets as good and a kind of justice we are in need of now.

The association of fairies with childhood then emphasises their role as a way of experience relating to innocence, rather than providing an escape from reality. This also happens in Rudyard Kipling's book *Puck of Pook's Hill* (1906), where Shakespeare's character appears to the children at the centre of the story. They are performing a child's version of *A Midsummer Night's Dream* within a fairy ring on midsummer's eve, and they do the whole thing three times. Puck himself then appears to them and wonders why they are surprised, given what they have been doing, explaining that the titular 'Pook's Hill' means 'Puck's Hill'. This re-enchantment of the fairy world comes with an explanation, however, when he explains that no one, none of the fairies, is left in the hills but him.

The whole book is about history and connection with place and the spirit of place, much as a psycho-geographer might want to do now, and amounts to a plea for the little place of imagination and enchantment from the beginning. Poems are interweaved in the book and 'A Pict Song' is about the ability of small things to affect the world powerfully. The whole of the book has a subtlety not often attributed to Kipling, or to fairy stories, who some see as only worth using to subvert.

Angela Carter's *The Bloody Chamber and Other Stories* (1979) is often held up as an example of how far you can go with the subversion of the fairy tale, but often, although she complicates and makes more realistic the tales she uses, she has respect for the originals and values them for themselves. Her version of 'Beauty and the Beast', for example, 'Mr Lyon', has subtle changes that reveal the psychology and emphasise the poetic resonance of the source. The stories remain about the sense of possibility in the magic of innocent imagination, which is in danger of being lost, along with the fairies.

There is evil in fairy tales too, and the wilfulness of fairies echoes our own struggles with ego and with control and power, but the sense of the possibility of transformation and the transformation of evil is never far away. The 'dark wood' offers good and evil but being found is never far from being lost. If we can reclaim the fairies, maybe they will reclaim us. To be away with the fairies might be a way to have our feet back on the ground of solid connection to the earth, as Kipling's Puck seems to suggest.

George Eliot's miserly bachelor Silas Marner, looking for his lost hoard of money, finds it replaced by a golden child, in an image of almost alchemical transformation and returning:

> When Marner's sensibility returned, he continued the action which had been arrested, and closed his door, unaware of the chasm in his consciousness, unaware of any intermediate change, except that the light had grown dim, and that he was chilled and faint. He thought he had been too long standing at the door and looking out. Turning towards the hearth, where the two logs had fallen apart, and sent forth only a red uncertain glimmer, he seated himself on his fireside chair, and was stooping to push his logs together, when, to his blurred vision, it seemed as if there were gold on the floor in front of the hearth. Gold!—his own gold—brought back to him as mysteriously as it had been taken away! He felt his heart begin to beat violently, and for a few moments he was unable to stretch out his hand and grasp the restored treasure. The heap of gold seemed to glow and get larger beneath his agitated gaze. He leaned forward at last, and stretched forth his hand; but instead of the hard coin with the familiar resisting outline, his fingers encountered soft warm curls. In utter amazement, Silas fell on his knees and bent his head low to examine the marvel: it was a sleeping child—a round, fair thing, with soft yellow rings all over its head. Could this be his little sister come back to him in a dream—his little sister whom he had carried about in his arms for a year before she died, when he was a small boy without shoes or stockings? That was the first thought that darted across Silas's blank wonderment. *Was* it a dream? He rose to his feet again, pushed his logs together, and, throwing on some dried leaves and sticks, raised a flame; but the flame did not disperse the vision—it only lit up more distinctly the little round form of the child, and its shabby clothing. It was very much like his little sister. Silas sank into his chair powerless, under the double presence of an inexplicable surprise and a hurrying influx of memories. How and when had the child come in without his knowledge? He had never been beyond the door. But along with that question, and almost thrusting it away, there was a vision of the old home and the old streets leading to Lantern Yard—and within that vision another, of the thoughts which had been present with him in those far-off scenes.

The thoughts were strange to him now, like old friendships impossible to revive; and yet he had a dreamy feeling that this child was somehow a message come to him from that far-off life: it stirred fibres that had never been moved in Raveloe—old quiverings of tenderness—old impressions of awe at the presentiment of some Power presiding over his life; for his imagination had not yet extricated itself from the sense of mystery in the child's sudden presence, and had formed no conjectures of ordinary natural means by which the event could have been brought about.

But there was a cry on the hearth: the child had awaked, and Marner stooped to lift it on his knee. It clung round his neck, and burst louder and louder into that mingling of inarticulate cries with "mammy" by which little children express the bewilderment of waking. Silas pressed it to him, and almost unconsciously uttered sounds of hushing tenderness, while he bethought himself that some of his porridge, which had got cool by the dying fire, would do to feed the child with if it were only warmed up a little.

(George Eliot, *Silas Marner*, from chapter twelve)

Write About

The fairies return – with positive help, or for revenge.

A fairy who personifies the promise of your childhood discusses the possibilities of promise in the world with you.

Puck explains why the fairies have departed.

'Has our Faust frightened our fairies away?' Read this and the previous chapter and write something with this title.

Fairies as alternative to today's world.

Fairy rings are a feature of natural fungal growth. Research their biological and folkloric histories and create a piece of writing, fiction or non-fiction.

Rewrite Richard Corbet's 'Farewell to the Fairies' for the modern world:

> Farewell, rewards and fairies,
>   Good housewives now may say,
> For now foul sluts in dairies
>   Do fare as well as they.
> And though they sweep their hearths no less
>   Than maids were wont to do,
> Yet who of late for cleanness
>   Finds sixpence in her shoe?
>
> Lament, lament, old Abbeys,
>   The Fairies' lost command!
> They did but change Priests' babies,
>   But some have changed your land.
> And all your children, sprung from thence,
>   Are now grown Puritans,
> Who live as Changelings ever since
>   For love of your domains.
>
> At morning and at evening both
>   You merry were and glad,
> So little care of sleep or sloth
>   These pretty ladies had;
> When Tom came home from labour,
>   Or Cis to milking rose,
> Then merrily went their tabor,
>   And nimbly went their toes.
>
> Witness those rings and roundelays
>   Of theirs, which yet remain,
> Were footed in Queen Mary's days
>   On many a grassy plain;
> But since of late, Elizabeth,
>   And later, James came in,
> They never danced on any heath
>   As when the time hath been.

By which we note the Fairies
　　Were of the old Profession.
Their songs were 'Ave Mary's',
　　Their dances were Procession.
But now, alas, they all are dead;
　　Or gone beyond the seas;
Or farther for Religion fled;
　　Or else they take their ease.

A tell-tale in their company
　　They never could endure!
And whoso kept not secretly
　　Their mirth, was punished, sure;
It was a just and Christian deed
　　To pinch such black and blue.
Oh how the commonwealth doth want
　　Such Justices as you.

Magical Texts and Literary Examples

Katherine Briggs. *A Dictionary of British Folk Tales* (1970).
Katherine Briggs. *A Dictionary of Fairies* (1976).
Angela Carter. *The Bloody Chamber and Other Stories* (1979).
Angela Carter (ed.). *The Virago Book of Fairy Tales* (1990).
Richard Corbet. 'Farewell to the Fairies' (1647).
George Eliot, *Silas Marner* (1861).
Joseph Jacobs. *English Fairy Tales* (1890, 1894; available online, as are Grimm's and many other collections).
Rudyard Kipling. *Puck of Pook's Hill* (1906).
A.E. Waite. *Fairy Music* (1888; original title *Elfin Music*).
Marina Warner. *Once Upon a Time: A Short History of Fairy Tale* (2014).
W.B. Yeats. 'The Stolen Child' (1886).

15

Childe Roland: Dark Towers, Slughorns and Oliphants

I remember students being set an essay with the question, 'What's wrong with Victorian poetry?' My feeling was that there was nothing wrong with Victorian poetry but that there was something wrong with us. At the time, this might have been a controversial point of view, but the noise of modernism, which is no longer even modern, now seems less pervasive. Mid-nineteenth-century gloom takes a lot of matching in my opinion and modernism owes much to it. The influence of the magical on such figures as Tennyson and Browning, not to mention Rimbaud, makes their gloom even more attractive to contemporary readers and especially to writers.

Robert Browning (1812–1899) wrote 'Childe Roland to the Dark Tower Came' in 1855 as a kind of dream, in the same way that George Eliot says she wrote *Silas Marner,* where she interrupted work on a longer novel to attend to this inspired work. Even for Browning, the poem is considered strange. Despite its distance of Victorian formality, its oddness, even its forbidding roman numeral verses, writers have been intrigued by it and he was frequently asked about it.

The poem, of thirty-four, six-line stanzas, is a kind of anti-epic. The quest to come to the gloomiest place and proclaim arrival is via the gloomiest journey. The anti-epic begins with the classic Mentor figure, the archetypal, older, helpful guide figure from the *Odyssey* being replaced by lies from a politically incorrect 'malicious' parody of a Janus threshold guardian, set only to mock rather than help or prevent entry. In stanza V, we even get an epic-style simile, but instead of being about the fierceness of a lion, as we might in a traditional epic, we get 'As when a sick man … ' listens, in stanza VI, to people talking about him as already dead.

Obviously an entry into an underworld, then, but this is even darker and starker for being epic-like, where lies replace the Muse and despair is where we start from. The only thing the quest seems to be about is an 'end' of some kind, as indicated in stanza III.

More waste than *The Waste Land* then, the poem prefigures all apocalyptic recent dooms, as it outlines lies, failure, sickness, nature made 'ignoble' and polluted, animal degradation, friendships betrayed, a poisoned river full of living dead, wars, monstrous machinery, the road behind disappeared into grey nothing, and the prospect of death. Match that (see 'Write About' exercises below)! The eerie atmosphere is unrelenting, the phrases relishing the grimness. The extremity is beguiling.

Being a liar too, rejecting success, wondering if he's even good enough to fail, only culminates in the blowing of a 'slughorn' to proclaim the slogan or title. As a vision of death and evil, you might think that enough, but Margaret Atwood claims the poem as an allegory of the darker side of writing. In *Negotiating with the Dead* (2002), republished under its easier subtitle 'A Writer on Writing', she says that the quest is the writing of the poem, which is actually then achieved. This is in her chapter 'Duplicity: the jekyll hand, the hyde hand, and the slippery double' where she insists on the underworld nature of creativity. The writer must deal with every despair, take it on, in order to test creation to destruction, so the picture of Roland as writer is another version of 'Thomas the Rhymer', who we encountered in Chapter 4 of this book. Later in the chapter Atwood says this is why you cannot actually know a writer at all, as they cannot take their dark duplicity on a book tour. As Browning writes, convincing us of Atwood's case, a writer has 'a life spent training for the site' of doom (stanza XXX).

The roots and sources make interesting connections to the dark, writer's magic of the poem. Reusing fairy tales and referring to them, we know from Browning, connect us with Shakespeare in his great play of despairs, *King Lear*, where Edgar, himself being a double of a Fool, quotes the line which culminates Browning's poem with its own title. This phrase echoes back and forward in literature. The 'childe' is interesting in itself, denoting someone noble but youthful, as a Knight in training, a parallel to the 'Jack' of fairy tales, where we get a similar picture of a sensitive, but not unresourceful young man. In the fairy tale 'Child Rowland', he is the youngest of three sons, archetypal for the less worldly, for the writer even. The 'dark tower' is not present in the fairy tale collected in the nineteenth century, except in the later version from Joseph Jacobs' *English Fairy Tales* (1890), where he restores it under Shakespeare's influence. The earlier one has a 'round green hill'. But Shakespeare must have known another version. The phrase has been used often, especially recently, and its sense of a kind of triumph of darkness, a kind of reaching of darkness towards heaven, could be seen to symbolise a power of death or evil, but also an attraction to it, or a watching out from it. As a symbol of creativity, then, it has the potency of the mysterious being elevated.

W.B. Yeats' final poem 'The Black Tower' (1939) seems related to the same tradition, where poor but devoted old men keep some tradition or faith going in the face of death. The bleakness and desolation are familiar to readers of Browning or the fairy tale, reaching forward to Bob Dylan's song 'All Along the Watchtower' (1968) where similar winds of change threaten. These all seem the same bastion of acknowledgement of death and doom in the magical defiance of art.

What might be more important is the verb aspect of the whole phrase, 'Childe Roland to the Dark Tower Came'. The approach, the attraction, the journey towards the implacable is the one that must be made. The final mysteries of life must be embraced with all the humour or horror that can be mustered.

The fairy tale offers more of a positive ending, where Rowland rescues his sister and two brothers who went before him and disappeared into the King of Elfland's world. Rowland spares his life after a fight, in exchange for this. There is more of an echo here of Orpheus rescuing Eurydice, although that is unsuccessful, or perhaps of Persephone being rescued from Pluto, where she agrees to spend half the year with him and half in the world above. There is a balance here between the two halves of the questing, rescuing Childe who restores something in the journey.

This is in contrast with Edgar in *King Lear* who pretends to be mad and gets a bit carried away with it, although he lives at the end of the play and is a bearer of the tale of Lear, so the comparison with the redeeming son is not lost. Even in Browning's dark tale, the humour, as in 'Thomas the Rhymer', is not gone. There is a test of madness for Edgar in his speeches, Browning in his extremity, as there is in the fairy tale, where

Roland almost forgets the warnings of having to kill those who speak to him on his way and especially the one about not eating or drinking in 'the land of fairy'. The comic madness is connected and part of the way of overcoming.

Browning does overcome, as Atwood attests, in writing the poem, in arriving at the place at all. Writers are forthcoming: their works are on the way, their journeys through the underworld have to be taken, however incapable they feel. This sense of life being hard to make from the materials available is heightened in the writer, but is shared.

Like the dark tower, the slughorn has proved resonant for other writers, notably J.K. Rowling has a character named after it. Thomas Chatterton seems to have invented the word and it has been suggested that it means 'slogan' in some kind of mistaken corruption. The oxymoron-like nature of sluggishness and blowing a slogan has an interesting parallel in the French medieval poem *The Song of Roland*, the eleventh-century battle epic, which has a few useful connections otherwise. Part of the battling hero's equipment is a similarly absurd instrument, called an Oliphant. This is a version of 'elephant' and means an elephant horn which can be blown. This Roland, having difficulty in battle, might summon help by blowing it, which he refuses to do.

'Sound the Oliphant!' they cry and he says 'Never!'; this happened several times and the unintended humour is compounded when, taking ages to die, he finally does blow it and bursts his head in the effort. Sounding the unlikely or absurd horn, 'dauntless', as Browning says, in the one positive word in his poem, seems central and vital, although the fairy tale has no mention of it. The fairy tale Rowland has to repeat a spell three times to open the door, which makes sense but the doomed horn is a beguiling blast.

Yeats' 'The Black Tower' also has a defiant horn, which only the 'cook' of the old knights of art can hear, and is then accused of lying, in a move slightly more bleak than Browning's. But the horn is that of the old king who is likely dead and gone, though it is reported as being 'great'. These are familiar themes in Yeats' poetry, as all is measured against the magic power of the past. It is a strange and mysterious final poem, where the darkness of the traditional tower of a kind of death-defiance has grown even darker and bleaker. The horn of art, however doubted, is still 'great'.

Wordsworth's sonnet, which begins 'The world is too much with us' (XXXIII; *c*.1802) is a lament for the growing materialism of the world and its 'sordid boon'. His calling on the image of the horn is more obviously positive, however. The last four lines of the sonnet culminate in the image of the horn:

> So might I, standing on this pleasant lea,
> Have glimpses that would make me less forlorn;
> Have sight of Proteus rising from the sea;
> Or hear old Triton blow his wreathéd horn.

Proteus is a God of the sea, who Odysseus has to wrestle to get an answer from, as the God changes shape at will. If you hang on, he will give you an answer. He is the ultimate protean (which is where that word comes from) mythic creature, the shape-shifter of myth and art. Triton is the messenger of the sea, a kind of merman with a fish's bottom-half, who uses his horn to calm or raise the waves. The sea here is like the dark of towers, the great unknown, with its powerful and prophetic creatures culminating in Triton, whose conch-shell horn is wreathed like the traditional crown of laurels worn by a poet. The symbolic horn is blown to command the magic of art.

Biblically, too, the horn is one of prophecy and power. The book of Joshua has him hearing from God in chapter 6, verse 5 about what will happen to Jericho. 'And it shall come to pass, that when they make a long blast with the ram's horns: and the seventh day ye shall compass the city seven times, all the people shall shout with a great shout; and the wall of the city shall fall down flat, and the people shall ascend up every man straight before him.' This then happens, when 'the seven priests bearing the seven trumpets of rams' horns' (verse 8) begin to fulfil the prophecy. The ritual opening up of a dark place, as in the fairy tale of Rowland, happens.

All these horns are then horns of the power of art, of defiance and of prophecy. Browning's prefiguring of the darker poetics of, say, *The Waste Land*, as well as more directly of pollution and despair, make him one with all these writers linking to these images.

The animal defence system, made of horn, giving music, borrows the animistic power with the dauntless trumpeting of art, while the note carries the wind of change into the future of its revelation. The ultimate positive image of the horn might then be the cornucopia, which derives from the Latin, meaning 'horn of plenty', which seems opposite to Browning, but not unrelated. One version of this story has the greatest Greek God Zeus as a child, being looked after by animals. He breaks off the horn of a goat, which from his power then becomes able to give endless nourishment, like a self-filling cup. The horn of plenty, containing all good things, is still used in folkloric festivals over the world as an image of abundance and plenty, an image of spring.

Non-existent slughorn to elephant, ram's horn to conch shell, goat horn or 'great' horn – all these are horns of the strength of the human imagination in physical form. And we have not even mentioned angels blowing horns: 'And he shall send his angels with a great sound of a trumpet, and they shall gather together his elect from the four winds ... ' (Matthew 24:31).

The blast destroys or defies, calls for help or proclaims glory, but it is near the place of potential death, and near the place of potential life.

Write About

Find a line in Shakespeare or another writer, or a quoted phrase which sums up something powerful and hard to understand, and devise a tale that leads towards that ultimate statement.

Match Browning's description of multiple negative things (as listed above).

Write about a writer's darker side coming out on a book tour.

What would your 'dark tower' be like?

'Burd' is a female equivalent of the male 'Childe', denoting a youthfully promising figure (as in the 'Childe Rowland' fairy tale). Write a dark quest from a female perspective.

Create a horn which has prophetic properties.

Cuthbert and Giles appear in stanzas XVI and XVII of Browning's poem:

XVI

> Not it! I fancied Cuthbert's reddening face
>> Beneath its garniture of curly gold,
>> Dear fellow, till I almost felt him fold
> An arm in mine to fix me to the place,
> That way he used. Alas, one night's disgrace!
>> Out went my heart's new fire and left it cold.

XVII

> Giles then, the soul of honour—there he stands
>> Frank as ten years ago when knighted first.
>> What honest man should dare (he said) he durst.
> Good—but the scene shifts—faugh! what hangman hands
> Pin to his breast a parchment? His own bands
>> Read it. Poor traitor, spit upon and curst!

Work out a version of their stories of epic failure (for example, see minor characters made central in the 'Creative Example' from Chapter 13, on Faust).

What would your own worst story be and how would you defy it with a 'dauntless' blast?

Act III, Scene iv of *King Lear* ends with the source of Browning's poem:

> 'Childe Roland to the dark tower came;
> His word was still, "Fie, fo and fum,
> I smell the blood of a British man"'

Imagine these words of a giant or King of the Underworld as denoting a fresh creative talent, hoping to write something good for the all-consuming dark of creative magic, as attempted in the poem below …

Creative Example

The Dark God of Magic Smells New Blood

Fee, Fie, Fo, Fum
Slughorn and Oliphant will forthcome
Fee, Fie, Fo, Fum
To quest addiction you'll succumb

Fie, Fo, Fum, Fee
Every journey ends with me
Fie, Fo, Fum, Fee
Doomed nascent creativity

Fo, Fum, Fee, Fie
How else will you prophesy
Fo, Fum, Fee, Fie
But through the lie which calls the lie?

Fum, Fie, Fee, Fo
Do you think you've got the cheek to blow?
Fum, Fie, Fee, Fo
Reach the Dark Tower, then you'll know

Fee, Fie, Fo, Fum
Blasted blowers, everyone –
Fee, Fie, Fo, Fum
Come on then, do you want some?

Magical Texts and Literary Examples

Magical

Margaret Atwood. *Negotiating with the Dead* (2002).
'Childe Rowland' in Joseph Jacobs *English Fairy Tales* (1890; available online).

Literary

Robert Browning. 'Childe Roland to the Dark Tower Came' (1855).
Bob Dylan. 'All Along the Watchtower', *John Wesley Harding* (album, 1968).
Shakespeare. *King Lear*.
The Song of Roland (c.1040–1115)
William Wordsworth. 'The World is too Much with Us' (c.1802).
W.B. Yeats. 'The Black Tower' (1949).

16

Magical Animals

In the blowing of horns in the previous chapter, we have already caught a glimpse of the animating force of our fellow creatures. Our relationship with them is a complex one and the various ways we relate to them tell us much about ourselves. The German poet Rilke advised a young poet to write about animals as a way of getting outside the solipsistic concerns of youth. Animals are our other selves in many ways, the otherness, the difference by which we can define ourselves. We envy animals their naturalness and their being so much part of the world of nature. They symbolise the instinctual, the aggressive, the in-tune; their sheer primitive power reminds us of what we are as well as what we are not. They return us to the body, to sex and mating, to what is stronger than our surface of ego, culture and rationality. The instinctive side of us reawakens. Encounters with animals make us feel alive, or shock us into being alive.

We make friends or food of animals, they guard us or threaten us. We wonder at their herding, flying and swimming, about their freedom or slavery. They connect us back to the elements, they level us to their level. When we are ill or well or eating, we know how animal we are and this can liberate us from vanity.

The natural history, the folklore and the symbolism of any animal can be good research for a writer, as can special feelings of attachment to particular animals. We attach all kinds of magic to animals, partly because they seem more connected to the strangeness and naturalness of the world. No doubt we project ourselves onto them and we use anthropomorphism, which is the false attribution of human qualities to animals, for both positive and negative ends. Animals connect us to a more primitive view of ourselves, so we read them as if messages from some deeper reality.

Animal guides are a popular element of shamanism, where particular strengths are attributed to animals, who might heal us, or act as our opposites to improve or rebalance ourselves.

There is a popular creative writing exercise which can give a writer an opportunity to find an animal 'other' to use for writing. A small group all write down what animal they would identify with each member of the group, including themselves. Each person notes down the animals attributed to them by each other member of the group, as well as their own. They then decide on an animal from their list to write about, somehow integrating some aspect of how they think about their own character. This exercise is not only instructive about how people think of each other, but allows writers to use an animal as a symbol.

A strong antipathy to, or identification with, an animal can make writing take on an aspect of the animal, like a spirit guide lending strength to a piece of writing. Animals themselves are fascinating, but animals as symbols make us part of them as well as seeing them as our 'others'.

The imaginary animal, or mythical beast, is another strong magical source for writing. These can be monsters which represent the Shadow archetype, or what we repress, or beasts with subtle qualities which represent something we have lost, as do the fairies (see Chapter 14), or unicorns. Mythology, bestiaries from history and invented beasts from Dante to fantasy are great source material. Jorge Luis Borges' *The Book of Imaginary Beings* (1967) is a terrific exploration of the topic. Combining the human with an animal can create an imaginary beast of one kind, but creating a beast which has supernatural elements, or a 'super' or different kind of consciousness, brings us towards science fiction as well as fantasy. We can embody qualities of immortality to the phoenix, or of elemental forces of destruction in the dragon. We find Gods in animals to challenge us, just as snakes were thought godly by their seeming ability to self-renew by shedding their skin.

Taking these imaginary beasts at face value can be a trap, but understanding them as aspects of the self can be useful to the writer. Having sympathy for their instinctive instruction can help them lend us their liveliness. Again, the key might be to find a mythical or magical beast with whom you identify and write from its perspective, where you will inevitably find yourself writing about your own self-insights.

Imaginary beasts can illustrate aspects of character which need to be addressed, as in Ovid's *Metamorphoses*, where the change makes the person into an embodiment of their passion.

The religious aspect of animals includes the idea of animism, which at a positive level is the belief that what animates matter is the life force or soul. This would include all of nature in it. The Egyptian belief that birds were the soul of humans who had left the earth is still a potent myth, as is the worship of animals in this context. All these are rich areas for writers. Also associated with the word, more negatively, is a belief in inanimate things having a soul, and a belief in spirits. Again, for writers, these are useful, not only in themselves but in a wider view which sees every detail as significant, as a writer tries to write the world into being.

In *Animism* (2005), Graham Harvey's subtitle makes the link with ecology – 'Respecting the Living World'. Seeing the world as essentially alive has always been essential to writers, however. It was the novelist William Golding (1911–1993), in discussion with scientist James Lovelock (b. 1919), who came up with the concept of Gaia, which treats the world as a living organism. Harvey's first epigraph for the book is from William Blake's 'Everything that lives is holy', which is the last line of 'The Marriage of Heaven and Hell'. All, including animals, are elevated to 'person' here, which is a liberating thought but not uncommon to writers. Think of *Animal Farm* (1945) by George Orwell. Paul Auster (*Timbuktu*, 1999) and Virginia Woolf have written novels where a dog is the narrator. The term 'anima mundi', meaning the soul of the world and associated with animism, is used by Yeats in 'The Second Coming', for example.

All this amounts to an associative, social view of the whole world as inherently having meaning. As I remember a friend of mine saying to me, when trying to explain the validity of magic, 'either the world has meaning, or it hasn't'. Graham Harvey's is a wider view of animism, as he is keen to point out how condescending, patronising and dismissive views of 'primitive' versions of religion were, as displayed by some early anthropologists. Writers, of course, would be interested in both, as we might imagine an anthropologist being persuaded against his intellectual judgement (see the 'Write About' section).

Perhaps in trying to describe other religious viewpoints, we have eventually invented a new religion for ourselves, one which challenges Western materialism. Harvey's book is inspiring and reminds writers what they must do to feel the significance of all that must be recognised as alive. Animal liberation is one of the energies behind such thinking, as illustrated in J.M Coetzee's novel *Elizabeth Costello* (2003).

Animal sacrifice is something which is associated with animism, where the life of the animal is returned to the Gods and thus 'made sacred', which is the meaning of the whole concept of sacrifice. In a positive way, the respect of hunters for the hunted can make death seem positive, although death is still our taboo today, however liberal we imagine ourselves to be. Animals are still the place we look to understand death, hunting and sacrifice.

Again connected with our unconscious or Shadow archetypal selves is the Jungian idea of the anima and the animus. These are, respectively, the unconscious female and male opposite sides of ourselves which give motivation to us through our symbolic relationships at a deep level. Our concepts of otherness, our Mother, Father, Wife, Husband and so on are seen here as key to balancing our own relationships in the world.

This kind of otherness as opposite is present in animals as archetypes. Tricksters are usually animal: coyote, or the sly and clever Reynard the Fox (see Chapter 6) and we are familiar with the lion as courageous or the intelligence of dolphins. History has projected all kinds of useful ideas onto animals and into imaginary animals, as mentioned above. Medieval bestiaries, which can be found online are great sources both of animal mythological traits and of imaginary animals.

Animals crossed with people can represent nature versus culture embodied. In the Greek tragedy *Oedipus*, the Sphinx is a woman with a lion's body and wings of a bird, who devours those who cannot answer a riddle. Mermaids are another hybrid creature and offer their mixed blessings. All these things offer a connection with the vitality of the living world of animals and the possibility of a reunion of the self with its vitality. They also reflect the inner life of the self and its desire to be fully expressed.

Talking animals are obviously projections of ourselves but also opportunities for the self to be other. Turning into an animal, like Actaeon who becomes the stag which he hunts, can be a reminder of our mortality but also a magical transformation to escape the narrow world of man, as in *Steppenwolf* by Hermann Hesse (1927). Here, the central character finds symbolic freedom in his identification with the beast.

The vastness of the topic is apparent, as is its richness. Folklore and natural history give us colourful material to work from and writers have written in every way, using the animating world of our others, our familiars. Magically, the idea of the familiar is particularly fruitful. In medieval witchcraft, this was an animal spirit helper, or demon, who provided the magic. Animals here are then more directly in contact with the invisible world of magic and could answer if bonded to the magician. Sometimes this was said to be achieved by mixing a drop of the magician's blood in the food of the familiar. The exotic names said to be given to familiars can be evocative. Matthew Hopkins, persecutor of women accused of witchcraft, in his pamphlet of 1647 'The Discovery of Witches' lists 'Vinegar Tom', who was a greyhound with a cow's head and 'Pyewacket', 'Gredigut' and so on.

Animals embody the four elements, in birds of air, fish of the waters, burrowers into the earth and dragons breathing fire or the phoenix rising from the flames. They are our familiars in more senses than one and they do our magic for us, reminding us of the life we seek to capture or liberate within us.

The love of animals gives means of expression to the inarticulate, which reciprocates in the same way. The company of animals, where tone rather than content of voice and loyalty seem to count, takes the edge off being human and being mired in human pettiness. Walt Whitman (1819–1892) expresses this in his long poem 'Song of Myself', section 32:

> I think I could turn and live with animals, they are so placid and self-contain'd,
> I can stand and look at them long and long.

> They do not sweat and whine about their condition,
> They do not lie awake in the dark and weep for their sins,
> They do not make me sick discussing their duty to God,

> Not one is dissatisfied, not one is demented with the mania of
> owning things,
> …
> Not one is respectable or unhappy …

Much of what we gain from animals is here, which is a perspective on ourselves and even a view of ourselves which makes us feel absurd.

Love of animals also includes their power. The poet Edwin Muir (1887–1959) wrote two poems about the mystical power of horses, one in his first collection and one published more than thirty years later; the first called 'The Horses' and the second called 'Horses', which has a post-apocalyptic theme, to be discussed in the Postscript of this book, which is about the future.

The ancient Muslim society known as 'The Brethren of Purity' published an encyclopaedia (from around the tenth century), which contains a fable of the complaints of the animals against humans. Animals, then, have always haunted our imaginations and reconnect us to life. From the smallest fly to the most powerful beast, they remind us of our connection to all things, where all things are base but also have a vital magic.

A link to the unsaid, to what is occluded, is present in the story which ends this chapter. 'The Oxen' by Thomas Hardy shows how humans invest Christian magic in the animal world and how they are present in our strongest magic:

The Oxen

Christmas Eve, and twelve of the clock.
  "Now they are all on their knees,"
An elder said as we sat in a flock
  By the embers in hearthside ease.

We pictured the meek mild creatures where
  They dwelt in their strawy pen,
Nor did it occur to one of us there
  To doubt they were kneeling then.

So fair a fancy few would weave
    In these years! Yet, I feel,
If someone said on Christmas Eve,
    "Come; see the oxen kneel,

"In the lonely barton by yonder coomb
    Our childhood used to know,"
I should go with him in the gloom,
    Hoping it might be so.

Creative Example

Girlie

When I was a young fellow, my girlfriend Vera had a cat called Girlie, who was anything but. Girlie was wild and fierce and would struggle, bite and scratch if you tried to pick her up or stroke her. In some moods she was playful, but she could turn, or re-turn, at any time to her feral state. Still, I was patient with her and she seemed to like me. I moved slowly if she was near me, avoided the challenge of her green eyes and blinked to show my unthreatening nature.

I should explain that Vera was a very nervous girl, who never really trusted me. She was very clever and we were great pals, but we never got to being more intimate somehow. This seemed to make her more nervous, as if I should be certain for us both in these matters. But no one can do that for long.

One evening, I was sitting in the sofa at Vera's house, waiting for her to come and join me to watch a film of a Neil Young concert. Girlie came in. I kept still, pretending not to notice her. Girlie climbed onto the sofa and onto my lap and settled down. No claws, just stillness. I felt blessed and after a long few minutes, I even moved my hand very slowly and she let me stroke her lovely black back.

As Vera arrived in the room, I told her, smiling, not to make any sudden moves. Vera looked amazed at the rare sight of a domesticated Girlie.

'Girlie,' she crooned, 'You love him!'

Vera turned very gently and walked towards us. Girlie seemed to notice her, leap up and streak through the open door all in a moment, and was gone. The end of love, I thought, realising the extra dimension of this at once.

We were never so close again.

I was thinking about Girlie a year or so later, when I passed a poor black cat, run over, dead. It lay by the roadside, still beautiful. I recalled someone I knew who had died recently. He had been a man of serious, passionate, wild opinion. I remembered my Mum's old cat who died so fiercely, as if angry with death, but had been so gentle in life. I wondered how Vera was, and Girlie too.

Write About

Do a version of the animal writing exercise, described at the beginning of this chapter, and work on deepening or extending your chosen 'other'.

Describe an encounter with an animal which is uncanny or uses some folkloric or natural history element. The BBC's Radio 4 series 'Natural Histories' is an excellent source and most episodes are available online at the time of writing.

Find an imaginary beast you like, via a work like Borges' *The Book of Imaginary Beings*, or look up 'A Medieval Bestiary' website. Then write a version of the being's tale set in a modern world.

Choose an animal to be your guide or familiar and imagine what they teach you.

Describe a talking animal-person encounter: mermaid, trickster, Green Man of ecology and so on.

Imagine being turned into an animal by an enchantment and how you might be released from this (like the Grimm's tale, number one, 'The Frog King').

Write about an animal who gives you something you cannot gain in the human world.

Write the story of a superior anthropologist who becomes an 'animist' (as discussed earlier in the chapter).

Magical Texts and Literary Examples

Magical

'Natural Histories' series. BBC Radio 4.
Jorge Luis Borges. *The Book of Imaginary Beings* (1967).

Fairy tales.
Greek myths.
Graham Harvey. *Animism* (2005).
Medieval bestiaries.
Venetia Newell. *Discovering the Folklore of Birds and Beasts* (1971).

Literary

J.M. Coetzee. *Elizabeth Costello* (2003).
Herman Hesse. *Steppenwolf* (1927; trans. 1929).
Poems by Ted Hughes, including *Crow* and 'The Thought-Fox' (1970; 1957).
D.H. Lawrence. *Birds, Beasts and Flowers* (1930).
Edwin Muir. *Collected Poems* (1965).
Ovid. *Metamorphoses*.
Walt Whitman. 'Song of Myself' (1892: section 32).

17

Love and Magic

In a world sceptical of the supernatural we increasingly rely on love to provide the magic, while at the same time seeming intent on removing the supernatural from it. This paradox gives an indication of the troubles of love, which can be useful to writers, but there are other troubles which make love troublesome as a subject. That said, the subject is impossible to avoid, as illustrated in the love of animals in the previous chapter. So big as a subject and so ubiquitous and our only way of increasing, it can seem that we are too close to see it clearly. It is impossible, and impossible to avoid – but the impossible is our subject here. Beyond spells to ensnare a lover and the seeking of a hint of who a future lover might be, we had best look to the myths of love for some clue as to its serious magic. But first the difficulties …

The poet Rilke, in his *Letters to a Young Poet* advises, in the first letter, the titular poet to avoid writing about love. Too much has been done and it is hard to say anything new. In other words the main problem is that of cliché. These shortcut phrases and words might be useful between lovers and enact a ritual of bonding in life, but to a reader they are dead and flat. A writer can mock them or play about with them to make the writing seem new, but this warning is worth heeding and might help lead us to devising new ways of writing about love.

A third danger, after the overwhelming nature of love and the cliché, is the fact that writing about love is not love. The writer is focused on the writing and not on the beloved. A fourth is that most writing about love is about its absence, or yearning for it, which is also not love. *Romeo and Juliet* is about the impossibility of love, while 'Shall I compare thee to a summer's day' is about the author toying with metaphorical devices. The troubles of love and writing are wonderfully evoked in William Blake's notebook poem, 'Never seek to tell thy love'.

> Never seek to tell thy love
> Love that never told can be
> For the gentle wind does move
> Silently invisibly
>
> I told my love I told my love
> I told her all my heart
> Trembling cold in ghastly fears
> Ah she doth depart
>
> Soon as she was gone from me
> A traveller came by
> Silently invisibly
> He took her with a sigh

Blake overcomes the dangers by talking about the difficulties, which is one strategy. He does this without descending into abuse of love, but rather attending to its mystery and its capacity to evade self-consciousness. There is an evasion of anything that might bind love to service of what is not itself love. The poem, though seemingly bleak and heartbroken, offers hope in the very freedom it describes, where love must transcend any insistence of words. Love retains its magic in its difficulty.

The Greek God of love, Eros, commands 'the gentle wind' in the story of his love for the human Psyche, so the poem could be about him, as the 'traveller'. The history of Eros reveals much about our relationship with love, as it has evolved.

Ann-Déborah Lévy, in her chapter 'Eros' from the *Companion to Literary Myths, Heroes and Archetypes* (edited by Pierre Brunel, 1996), identifies a split between Eros being a God of love or the force of desire. In Hesiod's *Theogony*, Chaos is first, then Gaia, which is the earth, which makes Eros the third great force in the creation of the world. The cliché is true here, of love making the world go round. Eros soon has too much power, which seems a universal theme of the magic of love, as the first children are monsters born of the earth and the sky. In some versions of the story of Eros, Zeus eats Eros and then power and love can be used in the world. Eros is a god that has to be contained and used. He is a winged, supernatural creature and a god of beauty and of nature, but becoming from the first more human and a source of trouble and dichotomy. Aristophanes shows him as being desirable in himself, as well as being a force. He is later associated with Aphrodite as she symbolises the fulfilment of desire.

Greek erotic poetry takes the desirability and force of Eros on, towards the depiction of him as a kind of cherubic child, of the kind we are familiar with from art. The element of cruelty comes in via poets like Sappho. Ann-Déborah Lévy reports that Plato's *Symposium* also shows the split. Eros is either the instinct to find one's other half, as Aristophanes says, or he is the demon go-between of gods and humans, associated with desire and therefore with property and poverty. Does love then become an initiation into something higher, some magic of Eros as God, or become a trite image of a plump boy with a bow and arrow, who wounds and misuses power? Is love lust or magic? Lévy wonders if Eros has been lost entirely to the humanising done to him in culture, but the banality of love seems always reaching for a higher meaning, a higher magic, however blindly. The balance of love seems easily lost and easily rendered tragic or banal. The magic of love remains elusive.

Eros, as Cupid, in the story of Cupid and Psyche, as told in Apuleius' *The Golden Ass* (second century), shows us an Eros (who has become the Roman Cupid) who remains supernatural, though personally involved in the human world. Psyche, which means 'soul', is a mortal but cursed by her extraordinary beauty to remain alone, as all are intimidated by her and the Goddess Venus sees her as a rival. Her father consults an oracle to ask what to do. The advice is to dress her as for a wedding and take her to a rock where she would be taken by a monster. They do this and she is taken away by the winds, but she wakes up in a beautiful place, looked after by invisible forces and is mysteriously made love to by an invisible lover who says that if she looks at him, he will vanish. She persuades him to let her visit her family but her two sisters are jealous and say her husband is a monster and she should kill him. She agrees but drops oil from a lamp on his skin by accident and he wakes and she sees that it is Cupid. He vanishes, taking her up as she hangs on, but then she falls to earth and wanders in search of him. She pays her sisters back and then goes through various tests and punishments, including a visit to the underworld and another symbolic death, via opening a box she has been forbidden to open by Venus as a final test/punishment. This sends her into a dark sleep. Cupid finds her and takes her to become immortal with him.

Love is shown here with all its problems as a kind of curse which is overcome by the risk of seeking the supernatural quality it demands, as the tale has a happy ending. The innocence of Psyche cannot be held, neither can the erotic force of Cupid prevail, but the balancing of the two can achieve a fulfilment through the tests and trials and retain something positive: a unity of the world and the divine. Jack Lindsay, in the introduction to his translation (1932), points out the threefold nature of the tale. The first stage is a blind dabbling with the divine, the second a kind of fall back to earth and suffering, the third is, through test and trials, a return to the good in a balance of innocence and experience. This has something of the classic three stages of initiation about it: a descent, a test and a return.

In section one of chapter four, entitled 'The Love-Death' of Joseph Campbell's *Creative Mythology* (1968), he identifies three elements of love, 'Eros, Agape and Amor'. The first two of these have been seen as opposites – lust versus universal love – while the third seeks a balance between the two. We could see these as connected to the split between innocence disturbed by lust, which is a kind of first stage, while through suffering a kind of good love is achieved like a balance.

Apuleius, the author of *The Golden Ass*, was someone who was known to be an initiate of the cult of Isis and wrote a *Discourse on Magic* to defend himself against accusation of the use of occult powers, so it is likely that these stages of initiation were known to him. Jack Lindsay also points out that the overall plot of the book echoes the internal tale of Psyche in structure.

Love must happen at the deepest level, where the hero, or heroine, is virtuous enough to see the Goddess, or God, and not be too dazzled or destroyed. We seek something superhuman, some magic through love and blame each other when it goes wrong from not being holy enough. But the fault is often in our own vanity, lust or ambition and our lack of depth. Joseph Campbell suggests this centrality in his great outline of the hero myth, *The Hero with a Thousand Faces* (1949).

When tales of love enter more into the merely human world, they tend to become tragic. The twelfth-century story of Tristan (which means 'sadness') and Isolde has magic and a magic potion but ends in sorrow. Like *Romeo and Juliet*, tragic love seems to be portrayed as love that is stuck at the first stage of innocence plunging into the danger of romance, as if that were an end in itself. The tragic end is a kind of human retaining of the innocence of love as a kind of fulfilment, or the only one possible in this world. The picture of love is one of transgression.

Tristan sets out from Cornwall to Ireland to seek a wife for his uncle and finds Princess Isolde, who nearly kills him, as he had killed her uncle. She finally nurses him rather than fighting him, and returns from Ireland with him. On the way, they drink a magic potion given by her mother the queen for the marriage with his uncle and this causes them to fall in love. The uncle suspects them and they run away but are caught. Tristan escapes and marries someone else, also called Isolde. When he is wounded he asks for the first Isolde. If she agrees to come, the ship that she travels on will have a white sail, if she refuses, a black. Tristan's jealous wife, watching for the ship, sees a white sail, but tells him it is black. Tristan dies of grief as does the first Isolde when she sees him.

The doubles in the stories, two deaths, two Isoldes remain a compounding, rather than a balancing aspect and the supernatural force or Eros in the love potion seems to condemn them further. Love endures, but in a sad form and a tragic one, remaining in its youthful form. Human love is seen to oppose all earthly and supernatural laws, though its source is acknowledged as supernatural.

Going back to the Roman writer Ovid, his tale of Narcissus and Echo is another interesting take on impossible love. Narcissus starts like Psyche, beloved but loving no one. His mother is told he will only live long if he never knows himself. He becomes a symbol of self-love and can only see himself. Echo, by contrast, is cursed not to be able to talk, except by repeating others' words, as she had been punished for deceiving Jove by telling him stories. She is too knowing and he is too innocent, so their tale is one of being stuck too much in the personal or the worldly. The balance between the self and other cannot be achieved and they are cursed by the gods not to attain love. Ovid put the two myths together, which was his original contribution, and the balance in the writing achieves a kind of tragic elevation in the mind of the reader. The vanity and self-doubt shown in Narcissus and in Echo are an indication of a kind of youthful, unbalanced love, which is again, tragic.

The myth makes us ask: are women still inclined to be too worldly, too influenced by fashion, for example? Are men still inclined to selfishness? Or is it the opposite? Like any good myth, these strange and stunted lovers pose more questions than they answer. They also echo the world of art, which can also be too inward looking, although Narcissus does turn into a flower, like a work of art. Echo could be someone who remains a voice but can only say what is already said. A tale of two writers suggests itself. Writers, like these two, give love out and are not rewarded in any direct way.

It is part of the curse of love for them that they know their problems. Echo, from the beginning, is aware of her curse, while Narcissus eventually learns that he is looking only at himself. Both are returned to nature in a way. The backstory of Echo is useful and is about storytelling and love, as is the frame story of the *Arabian Nights*, but in a more positive way. Scheherazade, in the *Nights* tells stories to stop herself being killed by her cuckolded husband the king who executes each of his wives after a single night of marriage.

In some earlier versions of Narcissus, his lover is a male who commits suicide, whereupon he himself goes the same way finally.

Narcissism is a well-known psychological state and the root of the name is the same as for the word 'narcotic', so Narcissus seems to rule the current world in some ways. Echo might be comparable to the internet, with its repeated bouncing of uninformed opinion – you could call it 'Echoism'.

We have been led, by old tales, into the labyrinth of the impossibility of love. Love needs a blessing of balance, an acknowledgement of mature, initiate's magic to give it the strength to endure. The dangerous powers, which can transform 'for better or worse' are obviously cited in marriage ceremonies, as is the three-act structure used in romantic comedy. The depth of love's dangers and magic are challenged by its everyday nature in the world, where people just get on with it. Love must insist on its simplicity, despite everything. The magic, the 'gentle wind' of the god of love is everywhere but delicate too and this is why it fascinates writers and will continue to do. Devising a real initiation into love is not beyond us, as the positive initiation of Cupid and Psyche suggests.

Russian novelist Turgenev's *Torrents of Spring* (1872) shows the protagonist torn away from an ordinary, innocent but homely prospective bride, towards an erotic and knowing, promiscuous wife of a friend, even though he knows he will regret it. A blessing and some peace come only at the end of the novel and the end of his life, when he meets his first intended bride and she offers a kind of forgiveness. Our human dilemma is his, to be unable to balance the innocent, communal love with the erotic. Thus love has much weight to bear in the world, torn between the public and the private, where no other magic is known.

One of the great collections of love songs in recent times is Bob Dylan's album of songs called *Blood on the Tracks* (1975). Known to be about the break-up of his own relationships, although it has songs of innocence, as well as of experience, the writing of it has a positive side. The songs were written, seemingly after a long decline in creativity in the writer's work, in a great flood of inspiration and are acknowledged as a return to form. Love and its dangers must have been a force in this, but Dylan also has mentioned his art teacher helping him to free up his instincts as a writer and to be able to do, consciously, what he used to be able to instinctively. In the rebalancing of his creativity, which has been through an innocence of flow, an experience of decline, then a reconciliation of the two, the writer has found a more positive way to write. The magic came back to Dylan, partly via love but partly through a maturation, which even seems to have later won him back the love of his life, which he had lost. Thus the final balancing stage of love's mature initiation is achieved.

The sacred conjoining or wedding blessed by supernatural means is portrayed in a key text for the Rosicrucians, *The Chymical Wedding of Christian Rosenkreutz*, published in 1616. This occult group named themselves after Rosenkreutz and the book was one of three founding documents of the movement. The mystical union of two persons is seen as the ultimate aim of magic and has inspired many writers and artists since that time. In the text, seven days' preparation are described, which has links to the creation of the world and to the Passover, as if holy love is a kind of re-creation. St Thomas' gospel (section 22), which reads like a poem, is often quoted in connection with *The Chymical Wedding*:

> When you make the two into one
> And when you make the inner like the outer ...
> And when you make the male and the female into a single one
> So that the male may not be male nor the female be female ...
> An image in place of an image
> Then you will enter the kingdom

Novelist Lindsay Clarke's *The Chymical Wedding* (1989) has a tale within its narrative about a couple attempting this 'great work', besides being a brilliant example of a contemporary work of fiction with magical themes. *The Purpose of Love* by Richard Gardner (1970) is a non-fiction book redolent of the 1960s interest in love as the great and magical goal of life, having a similar, positive, balancing theme. Here the magic of love is found.

The union of opposites which transforms, the power that holds the world together – love is all this, as much as it is powerfully dangerous magic. Eros the God is a primal creative force, manifest all around, which we must know. Love remains one of the main ways we break out of the ordinary world into the world of magic. Love and the writing of love are dangerous and powerful forces, which have the magic to transform, to create and make the world more magical.

Creative Example

If This Were a Romantic Comedy

If this were a romantic comedy
    There would be magic in the end
We would be transformed as one
    Not just a distant friend

A part of me, another self
    Writes in the dark alone
Of all the complicated truths
    Of where true love has gone

While the brighter me walks out
　　And feels the gentle wind
And blesses love in the simple high
　　Of any word that's kind

Write About

The 'Creative Example' poem above partly follows the three-part structure of innocent love followed by love being tested in the depths, then seeking a final union in some kind of universal or magical blessing, as does the Blake poem earlier in the chapter. Write something which follows this pattern, emphasising the alchemical union at the end.

'Love is so simple' is a phrase which is often quoted. Write of the simplicity of love in a complicated world. Use specific detail to avoid clichés and capture extremity of emotion.

Study the lyrics to 'Teenage Dirtbag', by Brendan Brown of the band Wheatus and try to use humour, narrative and mutual recognition of weakness or human frailty to create a transcendent love tale.

Write about a person as a place (a personification often used by writers of love songs).

Research the story of Psyche (or other mythical tales mentioned above) and write from her (or another's) point of view.

Write a modern Narcissus and Echo. One way might be to make them two writers: one too vain, the other too worried about being like everyone else.

Write about a present-day love potion, using some source material from one in literature (e.g. Tristan and Isolde, *A Midsummer Night's Dream*, etc.).

Write about a kind love that sustains – from your own life or imagined. How does the magic stay?

Magical Texts and Literary Examples

Magical

Apuleius. *The Golden Ass* and *Discourse on Magic*.
Joseph Campbell. *Creative Mythology* (1968).
The Chymical Wedding of Christian Rosenkreutz (available online).
Richard Gardner. *The Purpose of Love* (1970).
Ann-Déborah Lévy. 'Eros' from *Companion to Literary Myths, Heroes and Archetypes*
     (ed. Pierre Brunel; 1996).
Ovid. 'Narcissus and Echo' in *Metamorphosis*.
Tristan and Isolde.

Literary

William Blake. Notebook poems and *Songs of Innocence and of Experience*.
Lindsay Clarke. *The Chymical Wedding* (1989).
Bob Dylan. *Blood on the Tracks* (album, 1975).
Ivan Turgenev. *Torrents of Spring* (1872).
Wheatus. 'Teenage Dirtbag' (Brendan B. Brown, 2000).

18

Magic and Endings: Curses and Blessings

Write About: Five-minute Pre-exercise

For five minutes only, write using the title 'The End of Magic'. Later, see if you can connect what you have written to the themes of this chapter.

Beginnings are about us; endings are beyond us. Endings must still concentrate the mind, even as they remind us of what the mind cannot fathom. Writers must end things, must rehearse death, every time they finish a piece of writing, and some relish endings as a possibility of a lyrical flourish and some dread them as a trap – perhaps of cleverness or formulaic cliché – for the unwary. Endings have a magic which embraces the occult nature of acknowledging an end. Beginnings are significant and point ahead in a fateful manner; endings are fate itself.

We are haunted by endings and by death, as they have not only a fatal quality but also a moral force. Even the meaningless, which we might want to acknowledge, calls on us to make a rule from it. Our appetite for death has been discussed by psychoanalysis and philosophy. With the power to destroy the world, science has entered the magical realm of death. The book of Revelation, which ends the Bible, is full of death as a kind of ultimate inflation of the ego of humankind, satisfied in its destruction, which takes everything else with it. The outsider seems to crave attention by indiscriminate murder and religions of peace are used to justify killing of innocence. Yet death is seen as a last taboo, which we must respect with ritual, even in an age that might have sought to banish any superstition.

Everyone knows about the dystopian view of Aldous Huxley's *Brave New World* (1932), but few have read his later novel *Island* (1962), which is about dying well. *The Tibetan Book of the Dead* (trans. 1927) had a big influence on the culture of the 1960s, but is rarely discussed these days, though it is a guide to dying, as well as to living. Like the sacred marriage described in the previous chapter, this book describes a sequence of days, which again makes death a kind of beginning, a kind of creation. Ends are beginnings, as T.S. Eliot discusses in his long poem about such matters, *Four Quartets* (1944).

Ritualising death seems necessary, even in a non-religious society. People must get together to pay respect to that which is mysterious to them but which affects them powerfully. Like love, death has become the final place of ritual in the 'rational' West, where we must stand on the place between past and future and see the darkness around us in order to feel part of some kind of cycle of life. Endings are a powerful call to magic.

Charles Dickens' last words were a joke about death and the black humour of death is part of it, as any emergency worker will tell you. When told he should lie down, Dickens was reported as saying, 'Yes – on the floor.' This joke recognises that his illness had him at a disadvantage and his dramatic summing up of this seems worthy of one of his characters. Writer and poet Clive James' recent works on his own decline show a similar openness in wit to the great unknown.

The cliché paradox of a condemned man eating 'a hearty breakfast' is comparable to the kind of recognition and grim humour in the 'memento mori', or reminder of death, often a skull, which goes back at least to Elizabethan and even further to Roman times. The final flourish of life in the face of death, as some fruit trees are said to perform, is a known phenomenon. Death reminds us to live.

The traditional English folksong, the 'Lyke-Wake Dirge', especially in the version recorded by The Young Tradition in the 1960s, is thrilling and sombre, as well as accusing, and has the power of finality about it:

Lyke-Wake Dirge (seventeenth-century, or earlier, Yorkshire dialect traditional song)

This ae nighte, this ae nighte
Every nighte and alle
Fire and fleet and candle-lighte
And Christe receive thy saule

When thou from hence away art past
To Whinny-muir thou com'st at last

If ever thou gavest hosen and shoon
Sit thee down and put them on

If hosen and shoon thou gav'st nane
The whinnes sall prick thee to the bare bane

From Whinny-muir when thou may'st pass
To Brig o' Dread thou com'st at last

From Brig o' Dread when thou may'st pass
To Purgatory fire thou com'st at last

If ever thou gavest meat or drink
The fire sall never make thee shrink

If meat or drink thou ne'er gav'st nane
The fire will burn thee to the bare bane

This ae nighte, this ae nighte
Every nighte and alle,
Fire and fleet and candle-lighte,
And Christe receive thy saule

The reminder to live here is a reminder of the need to give to others and thus of certainly Christian, and possibly pagan charity. 'Whinnies' are thorns, which is a local as well as a Christian symbol.

The 'metaphysical' poets are seventeenth-century writers, like John Donne, who have wide and often magical concerns and conceits in their work, beyond the merely physical. Henry Vaughan (1621/2–1695) has an extraordinarily positive view of death in his poem beginning 'They are all gone into the world of light!':

They are all gone into the world of light!
    And I alone sit ling'ring here;

Their very memory is fair and bright,
  And my sad thoughts doth clear.

It glows and glitters in my cloudy breast,
  Like stars upon some gloomy grove,
Or those faint beams in which this hill is drest,
  After the sun's remove.

I see them walking in an air of glory,
  Whose light doth trample on my days:
My days, which are at best but dull and hoary,
  Mere glimmering and decays.

O holy Hope! and high Humility,
  High as the heavens above!
These are your walks, and you have show'd them me,
  To kindle my cold love.

Dear, beauteous Death! the jewel of the just,
  Shining nowhere, but in the dark;
What mysteries do lie beyond thy dust,
  Could man outlook that mark ...

These first five stanzas give such a wide perspective, reminding us of the mix of science and magic Shakespeare seems also to call on. The 'high Humility' is breathtaking and seeing the world as shadow and death as light has a similar exhilarating paradox at its heart.

Writers strive for these depths and effects. In 1960s the Beatles recorded 'Tomorrow Never Knows', which is based on a version of *The Tibetan Book of the Dead*, published in 1964, called *The Psychedelic Experience* by Timothy Leary, Richard Alpert and Ralph Metzner, and reads like an instruction for meditation, as well as a journey into the great unknown. The song, from *Revolver* (1966), where it is the final track, is all on one chord and has a hypnotic effect. The title is a kind of joke, comparable to 'A Hard Day's Night'. The mix of doom and exaltation is again present.

The ultimate reminder of the shortness of life might be the poetry of *The Book of Common Prayer*, from 'The Burial of the Dead', originally published in 1549 and edited by Archbishop Thomas Cranmer:

> Man that is born of a woman hath but a short time to live, and is full of misery. He cometh up, and is cut down, like a flower; he fleeth as it were a shadow, and never continueth in one stay.
>
> In the midst of life we are in death: of whom may we seek for succour, but of thee, O Lord, who for our sins art justly displeased? ...
>
> I heard a voice from heaven, saying unto me: Write: from henceforth blessed are the dead that die in the Lord.

Psalm 39 from the burial service has the line 'for man walketh in a vain shadow', which is reminiscent of Vaughan's 'world of light', which is death. These dark blessings also come into a more recent elegy, Dylan Thomas's 'Do Not Go Gentle Into That Good Night' (1951), where the narrator's father is asked for both blessing and cursing.

The two characteristics of the magic in endings tend to be blessings and curses and sometimes the oxymoron of both opposites together. The end section of Jack Kerouac's *On the Road* (1958) reads like a prayer, with a sunset setting, a repeated summoning up in a summing up of his main character, whose name is repeated three times in blessing. Likewise, James Joyce's *Ulysses* (1922) ends with the monologue of Molly Bloom, who repeats the word 'yes' like an invocation between phrases.

D.H. Lawrence's 'The Ship of Death' (1932) has a flowing celebratory feel in its sense of surrendering to the inevitable.

The most well-known curse-ending, however, occurs in the final book of the Bible. The book of Revelation was written in a dark time and its eschatology, which means the discussion of last things, is compelling and has an atmosphere of extremity. Here is the end of the last book:

> 13 I am Alpha and Omega, the beginning and the end, the first and the last.
> 14 Blessed are they that do his commandments, that they may have right to the tree of life, and may enter in through the gates into the city.

15 For without are dogs, and sorcerers, and whoremongers, and murderers, and idolaters, and whosoever loveth and maketh a lie.
16 I Jesus have sent mine angel to testify unto you these things in the churches. I am the root and the offspring of David, and the bright and morning star.
17 And the Spirit and the bride say, Come. And let him that heareth say, Come. And let him that is athirst come. And whosoever will, let him take the water of life freely.
18 For I testify unto every man that heareth the words of the prophecy of this book, If any man shall add unto these things, God shall add unto him the plagues that are written in this book:
19 And if any man shall take away from the words of the book of this prophecy, God shall take away his part out of the book of life, and out of the holy city, and from the things which are written in this book.
20 He which testifieth these things saith, Surely I come quickly. Amen. Even so, come, Lord Jesus.
21 The grace of our Lord Jesus Christ be with you all. Amen.

The 'Alpha and Omega' are the beginning and the end of the alphabet and there is no mistaking the condemnation of magic, which is 'without' with the 'sorcerers'. Yet the sorcery of cursing anyone who adds to or takes from the text is all too present. Try that in your creative writing assignment! In fact, this kind of curse at the end of a text was not uncommon at the time – editors beware! The fourteenth-century religious text *The Cloud of Unknowing* has a similar admonition at its beginning, suggesting how you read it.

It is hard to get away from the curse or blessing in the face of the unknown, as big questions demand big answers and a summing up become a summoning up of life force, where 'a Voice' says 'Write'.

One purpose of this kind of ending is to get rid of evil and gather hope. End-of-year ceremonies often involve a ritual burning, sometimes of a devil, for example, in Guatemala City. The concept of the 'sin-eater' is another way of the ridding of evil. In this a living person would take on the sins of the dead, in a kind of 'scapegoat' ritual. In Hertfordshire bread and beer were passed across a body to the 'sin-eater', who would be paid. This 'out-with-the old and in-with-the-new' ceremony helps turn the world, like the cry of 'Happy New Year'.

Even the banality of ending, as illustrated in Peter Cook's sketch for *Beyond the Fringe*, is a kind of triumph over it. Here, in 'The End of the World' (1961) a millennial cult assemble to watch the end of the world, chanting and prophesying. When it does not happen they all agree to meet the next day. The impossibility of endings is made manifest, as is the tendency for humans to want to dramatise. This end has proved popular and has been performed many times with success.

We revolt against ending, as Tennyson does, through 'Ulysses' (1842), in that great poem: 'How dull it is to pause, to make an end.' The line echoes its content, and the poem's subject, pausing and ending. We fear stasis so we need the bang of an ending, even if the real end is a whimpering, as T.S. Eliot describes it at the end of 'The Hollow Men' (1925), but the bravery of his honesty is actually a bang of an end.

The kind of honesty of ending is exemplified in Charlie Chaplin's film *The Great Dictator* (1940), where Chaplin breaks out of character and out of frame to address the camera and audience directly as himself. This moving speech for humanity and peace was so popular that people had it printed and framed on their walls at the time. Writers relish the change of gear, the inherent drama of endings. Chaplin's call for peace and equality still feels like a controversial move and he resisted opinions that it would not work at the time. An end must haunt us, like a song. An end is something to take away.

It is also difficult to end without seeing something beyond, which is a kind of religious thinking of a world destroyed to be renewed. The book of Revelation is again the prime example. In John Gray's *Black Mass* (2007), he describes the Christians George Bush and Tony Blair, at the time of the Iraq War, as having this kind of apocalyptic thinking behind it, consciously or unconsciously. It seems that we are inclined to believe in something beyond.

Few of us would want to write a curse ending, because for a writer, for a reader, endings have magic. The kinds of curses spread anonymously on the internet attest to this power, as they do great damage and have been known to ruin people's lives. The power of the word is misused but writers tend to respect the magic and might only perform a curse as a kind of joke or just protest or literary flourish of truth or revealing. The power of ending is the fear of death.

In *Primitive Mythology* (1959: chapter 2, vi), Joseph Campbell talks of a kind of archetype called 'King Death' and of Jung's belief that it is best to think of death as a kind of transition rather than an end. It is healthy, even without understanding, to see ends as beginnings, so as to aim for maturity, rather than fearing the great change that must come.

If that was my last paragraph of this section, you will have seen how I could not resist being dramatic, as now I am not resisting being honest, which is a different form of drama.

Write About

Imagine an apocalyptic scenario and write a curse or blessing ending for it.

Re-examine an ending you admire and emulate it in some writing, adding more magic/curse/blessing elements to it.

Ending can involve reversals or move towards an opposite, or repetition, or variation of a beginning. Create a piece of writing which uses this type, or one of these types, of ending.

Using a piece of writing you have already created, try a new ending which 'breaks the frame' and gives a new honesty or revelation to the original work.

Using the examples above, create a positive song about death, which nevertheless tells of its reality.

Magical Texts and Literary Examples

Magical

The Book of Common Prayer (1662).
The Book of Revelation in the King James Bible.

Timothy Leary, Richard Alpert and Ralph Metzner. *The Psychedelic Experience* (1964).
The Tibetan Book of the Dead (sixth century).

Literary

The Beatles. 'Tomorrow Never Knows', from *Revolver* (album; 1966).
Charles Chaplin. *The Great Dictator* (film; 1940).
Jack Kerouac. *On the Road* (1957).
D.H. Lawrence. 'The Ship of Death' (1932).
Dylan Thomas. 'Do Not Go Gentle Into That Good Night' (1951).
Traditional. 'The Lyke-Wake Dirge'.
Henry Vaughan. 'They are all gone into the world of light' (1665).

Creative Example

End Story

It was a normal day and I cycled the half-mile home to my house. I stopped twenty yards or so short, as an ambulance pulled up by my front door. My neighbour opened my front door and let them in. None of them turned my way and my neighbour went back into her house without looking round. I stood there, holding my bike. I don't know why I didn't move. A couple of minutes went by and the ambulance crew, a man and a woman, came out bearing a stretcher. Without seeing clearly, I had an instant and vivid sensation of absolute recognition. The person on the stretcher was me.

The ambulance drove away, as I stood there still. It was only then, as I went into my small house, that I doubted what I knew. I put my bike by the shed and went through the back door, which I always left open anyway. I sat on the sofa and doubted my own life, my own death. I thought I would try to phone Maggi G, as she was someone who could answer such a daft but fundamental question. I heard the dialling tone and dialled the local number, but nothing happened. The dial-tone continued. Strangely calm, I went out and tried to ring my neighbour's doorbell. Nothing.

After a while, she came out of the door as I stood there and didn't seem to see me at all. I spoke and heard myself, but was also aware that no sound came from me. The material world has ceased to register my presence. For some reason I checked my bike, to see if I had really ridden it home, but could see no evidence one way or another. I could move it, I found, but when I looked back at where it was, it was still there, too. Putting it there must have been final or coincidental to death.

After that, it seemed easy to accept that I was dead. That was the surprising part. Having accepted it, I found it terribly difficult to acknowledge the isolation I felt. In life there are many kinds of loneliness, but the loneliness of death was unbearable. I then began travelling and I cannot tell about how or where but ages and distances were so huge to me as to make me feel relieved, but at the same time more lonely than ever, or forever.

I returned to my spot of watching the house again to see some house clearance or other men, in brown coats, which I thought curiously old fashioned, emptying books from my house. I had a large collection of esoteric books. The carrying out of these to a van I found curiously satisfying, like a hygienic exercise. I found I could still remember each book I had read, with a kind of photographic memory which I did not have in life.

Dead people cannot write themselves but I remembered a spell that was not automatic writing of the kind practised by W.B. Yeats' wife, but a method of obtaining 'apported writing', which appears as if from nowhere. You may have read this book yourself. This section was said to be nonsense at the time, as were other parts of the book, which was called *Beyond the Magic of Writing*. All I can say is that it is connected with the weather and with the movement of light, which the dead can control, given certain conditions. The book's version does not in fact work. This section was written by an 'apport' or sudden appearance itself, but could only work from the position of someone already beyond the physical. Here is the paradox of magic.

This story is a message to Maggi but I cannot resist an end message, which is a common one which an older person will often say to a younger. Other than this, I have no great farewell:

Decide to be happy, to love one another and flourish.

This story was found imprinted, as if by light, on a few pages of Maggi G's shopping list pad, which hung from a string on the kitchen wall of her house in Balestead, Essex.

Postscript: Magic and the Future

Science fiction is the place where science and magic meet, bringing to mind the old conflicts and dualities between nature and God, poetry and philosophy, rationality and the imagination, and old dream of unity as a view of a future where the limits of the past are overcome in a kind of return to Eden. The dividings and unifications, cycles and returnings give us a sense of the future as somehow available to us. Just as endings are beginnings, endings are then calls to the future, where some new Fall calls for a new Return.

The picture of the future as a projection of now comments on how things are today. They present an occult view, a revelation of what is hidden. The warnings of the triumph of science are many and varied, but one of the most haunting in its relevance to the twenty-first century is one written over a hundred years ago by an author more associated with portraits of empire and society, of costume drama even, E.M. Forster. 'The Machine Stops' (1909) presents a world where nature has been abandoned, where people live inside the earth in isolation, their whole lives catered to by 'The Machine'. Their bodies are unfit for outside non-conditioned air and they communicate through devices only, listen to lectures and worship 'The Book of the Machine'. Everyone has thousands of friends who they never meet, everywhere is the same and they are horrified by sunrises, which they never normally see and by meeting anyone face-to-face. Remind you of anything?

The title tells the story. A son in the tale wants to see his mother face-to-face and she eventually travels by air, against all her better thoughts, finding the journey over the earth devoid of ideas and hateful. He wants to go outside, which is against everything they believe in, almost unthinkable. He eventually does this and battles with worm-like repair machines from inside but sees some outside renegade, 'Homeless' people living above ground. In part III, the Machine becomes a religion and then begins to break down. He manages to meet and kiss his mother. Mankind dies in and by the world, or the technology, they have made.

Inside the world seems to be a metaphor for our increased isolation from the world and each other, as well as an alienation from nature, but the magic must return, bringing a new person who wants to connect with a kind of unity through nature, towards a new Eden. Magic, as a desire for reconnection, asserts itself as the future.

The optimism of magic is something that it has in common with science. The nineteenth century gave rise to advances in science, but also to great studies in the occult. The 1960s, as discussed in Chapter 10, were another time when the future seemed to offer an expansion of the mind as well as technological advance. The end of the twentieth century seemed to turn away from open discussions of these potentials, but they are not so easily dispelled. The recent return of interest in nature writing and psycho-geography shows writers integrating mysticism and materialism in a grasp towards a balanced future.

French novelist Michel Houellebecq's recent work has concerned itself with futures, with religion, with the disillusionment and despair of the Western world. His controversial reputation has all the atmosphere of the accused magician about it, culminating in his novel *Submission* (2015). This was published on the same day as terrorists killed workers at a satirical magazine, while the novel depicts a future where an Islamic government rules France. His deep examination of the extremes of the human project seem to have reaped him the whirlwind awarded to, or reserved for, those who touch a prophetic nerve in the culture. As Jesus said, 'A prophet is not without honour, but in his own country, and among his own kin, and in his own house' (Mark 6:4).

When writers are serious, they seek to reveal something occluded in the world and bring its revelation to our attention in a way acceptable or recognisable. So we can then claim that all serious writing is not only magical but also prophetic. As I heard Dudley Young, author of the inspiring book *Origins of the Sacred* (1991), tell a class on Yeats and writing, 'Your job is to turn dream into prophecy'.

Recent writers on the occult have begun to reclaim the ground for serious examination and they also seem to emphasise the connection with the literary imagination. Jeffrey J. Kripal's *Authors of the Impossible* (2010) is written in a relaxed, at times jokey, tone but has an academic and serious persuasiveness at its heart. He points out in his introduction that there is a great thirst for magic in the world, as well as many examples of 'the impossible'. However, the topic is banished from any serious study. Our cultural landscape is full of magic, which we ignore. Given the massive influence of magic on literature, I would argue that this is even more anomalous in the study of literature and especially in the study of creative writing.

The 'authors' in Kripal's title are those who bridge the gap between magic and science and have revealing elements in common. These are writers on the occult such as Frederic Myers and Charles Fort, who have been left out of the picture of serious enquiry. The fashions of study have dominated and the ubiquity of the paranormal has been ignored and this situation is the same in science as it is in religious study and philosophy, which is Kripal's own field. Something that tends to happen is that truly original thinkers have an interest in these matters, which is later ignored by subsequent people who build on their work. The accusation of 'primitive' as a way of ignoring magic has been replaced by dismissing examples as merely anecdotal.

The idea that magic is truth, but a kind of literary truth, which therefore might be deeper, will not be an unfamiliar one to readers of this book. The implications of Kripal's arguments for a different kind of truth are truly significant for writers. Testing magic in the laboratory is absurd, as it is the wrong kind of test. Writing makes the impossible possible, you might say. It bridges the gap between the material world of consciousness and the world of the unconscious.

The scepticism of science thus becomes a kind of publicity triumph, while the ridiculing of 'New Age' ideas is an easy target. Thus we ignore what is inevitably inside us and part of our world, albeit occluded. In his conclusion, Kripal indicates a reactive swing towards taking magic seriously which seems to be beginning. The rich, oppositional nature of magic will begin to have some purchase. What the imagination creates is a significant part of our reality and culture, and cannot be left out of the picture.

There is a sense here of tuning into something, rather than feeling we are self-generating machines. In other words we are written, but we can also write. There is a creative optimism, a looking to the future in the whole book. Gary Lachman has a similar upbeat message in *A Secret History of*

Consciousness (2003), where he indicates that negativity about consciousness has produced an opposite effect in his own work. Significant scientists have said that there is no such thing as consciousness anyway, and many books and papers have been produced to reduce it to mere mechanics. The absurdity of this position calls for a re-examination of the whole history of the subject.

Lachman's book outlines theories of consciousness that do not leave out the magic. Like Kripal, he finds writers on this 'secret' aspect of the mind have much to tell us. No one is qualified to dismiss consciousness as mechanical and what science leaves out offers insights into the exploration of, and attention to, alternative views. Again, like Kripal, Lachman does not want to leave science out, but to expand its scope.

For writers, these ideas are full of justification of the creative position and the thinkers they explore are good subjects in themselves and in their ideas, which feel expansive and connected. The sheer usefulness of these ways of thinking for writers has been demonstrated and writers' connection to this other tradition cannot be overemphasised.

Science, you might argue, has made prophecy easy. Forster's story of domination by mechanical thinking has weight, as it merely projects a tendency to its logical conclusion. On the other hand, the way in which science has become destructive, almost unconsciously being our Promethean glory and doom, is the story with which we must grapple. The problem of prophecy is always that of being believed, as mentioned above in relation to Michel Houellebecq. Science, like magic and religion, has moved, with its world-destroying power, into the mythic and taboo. The significant and difficult matters of human existence and balances between good and evil are old questions which prophecy can address.

Prophets are set apart, like Tiresias in his blindness, with second sight, or Cassandra with her curse to tell truth which is not believed. Prophets embody the taboo. Part of the way to write prophecy is to enact this taboo of separation. Two favourite poems which have a prophetic element are Matthew Arnold's 'Dover Beach' (1867) and W.B. Yeats' 'The Second Coming' (1919). Looking at the structure of the two poems, a pattern begins to emerge.

The first move is a withdrawal from the world, or a kind of overview from a vantage point or place of reflection. The move away seems to find a perspective. In Yeats it is a sky view, in Arnold a view over the sea, but the bigger picture and the place of view seems key here, in their opening stanzas.

The second move is to evoke the past and/or reflect on the present world and its follies and relate the two. Arnold goes back to Sophocles and 'the turbid ebb and flow/of human misery', while Yeats sees disorder and recalls the notion of his title, 'The Second Coming', evoking large-scale views of the world spirit. Past and present, human yearning and failure, infect each poet with a kind of sad wisdom.

The third and final move is a projection into the future via the vantage point and the overview of the human world. Arnold sees individual love as being the only thing that will matter: 'let us be true/To one another' for the 'world' offers nothing now of the title's unity. Yeats is more directly prophetic, where he sees something monstrous replacing the hope of his title.

Both these poems are often quoted and have had a life beyond their time, and are inexhaustible in meaning and resonance. Both write about their prophetic moves in a personally engaged and direct way and draw the reader into sharing their vision, so that we see what they see. Both, in this sense, are about writing. The earlier poem is less conventional in structure but both have a lyrical and rhyming appeal and, in each dark vision, offer a kind of transcendence from it, which means, again, they are about magic or prophetic writing and function as a kind of spell of rebalancing the world.

Nostradamus (1503–1566) is possibly the most famous predictor of the future, although it is worth pointing out that there were others around at the time, who possibly remain largely unexplored and certainly less well known. He was a doctor in the plague years and was drawn to studying other prophets and to draw on their work. He set out to write one thousand obscure rhymed quatrains, which have always needed interpretation but have been widely quoted and wondered at.

His withdrawal then, echoing the above prophetic sequence (withdrawal, evocation, projection), was into a kind of learned obscurity, but he also seems to have used what sounds like meditation techniques to quieten the mind. If we think of his studying and use of older prophecy, we could equate that to the second stage, which leads to the accumulation of the vision of the future, which is stage three.

The Greek oracles featured originally a withdrawal by breathing in some kind of vapours from vents in the ground and thus make their withdrawal from the world via drugs, which then led them into answering questions. The questions often seem to embody human folly and the answers were sometimes trickster-like, riddle-like and strange. The mythological figure of Pandora, which means 'all gifted', comes into the world with the future in a vessel, which contains all the worst things that plague humankind. Only hope is left in the vessel, often called a box, but nearer to a jar perhaps. Gifts are like prophecies and hope is ambiguous and could be false. Pandora is the future, offering everything and nothing, a kind of troubling image like the kind that Yeats saw in 'The Second Coming', where our unity is a vision of disunity. Pandora is the end of the ambitious story of Prometheus, who cheated the Gods. His and Pandora's tale show a view that sees back into their story in a prophetic manner, like Adam and Eve, whose departure is a kind of backwards, three-move, prophecy.

Forster's story 'The Machine Stops', like many futuristic tales, seems to end with a departure, or the kind of withdrawal to a vantage point discussed above. Another thing that his tale has in common with Arnold and Yeats in their two poems is a concern for a wider world, a unifying vision, even if it is of disunity. But the key is that prophecy seems to ask for the possibility of a kind of unifying vision.

Joseph Campbell, in 'The Occult in Myth and History' (1977), from *The Mythic Dimension* (1997), offers the example of risking life to save another as a vision of the kind of unity which underlies our existence, which is the real meaning of what is 'occult'. This is the normally hidden fact that we are all part of each other under our superficial masks of individual consciousness. The other aspect of this hidden unity is revealed through the timeless, or the illusion of time. Again, all the works discussed above, inevitable in looking to the future, seek an overview of time in order to transcend it and offer this occult unity. This can be called the immanence: the inherent, pervading spirit of underlying oneness. Prophecy always calls on this, as, in a sense, all writing does, as it steps aside from direct life.

Kripal and Lachman seem to suggest that if consciousness is not physical, then the timeless unity of life seems more real, which is the tradition of magical thought, as opposed to science. Do we live on the surface of our limits? Forster's view in the machine-driven world is that we are in thrall to the limited view of our technology, where we are reduced to seeing everything flattened to two dimensions.

Does writing do this? Is writing a prophetic withdrawal or a reduction to a surface, to one dimension? The occult depth of writing is a potential. It is a sacred space where the correct ritual can produce the vision of the timeless unity in the future, where all things are revealed.

Magic reveals what needs to be hidden for the world to turn, but finally calls us back to the simplicities of unity and the possibilities of a deeper communication. The materialistic view of the world diminishes in the timeless, or depth, views of humankind, where the possibility of the future opens up like a prophetic vision.

Creative Example

A Study of Mind-Reading Habits

I was standing in Onego supermarket sweeping the place with my mind for thoughts, even though most people wore blockers. People like me who could bypass anything and see anyone's thoughts tended to keep it secret. I kept thinking of the bit in *Gulliver's Travels* where some people are so inside their own heads that they have to have attendants hitting them with bladders to keep them attached to the real world. When mind-reading became something anyone could learn, it seemed like the world had turned on its head, really literally – switched on its connected head to everyone else. It offered real promise: a promise of unity and understanding.

Occult powers coming true of course could go either way. In Christopher Priest's novel *The Glamour*, the gift of invisibility became a kind of addictive curse, making those who could do it outsiders. In the country of the blind the one-eyed man is king, as H.G. Wells and the Bible said. But mind-reading as a teachable skill changed everything. The public world, disappearing so fast, had returned. The ravers who danced all night, ecstatic, were correct: we are all one. But, obviously, people had tried to make money from it. Internet tycoons were scared by it, as their control methods were laid bare, but they adapted by trying to control it. They sold the blockers and blocker apps everyone used, though some of them did not work at all. Like that man who sold bomb detectors that did not work. In other words the world tried desperately to return to its messed-up ways. Mind-stalking became a problem, as did direct-mind advertising. New barriers were created to replace what the occult had hidden for so long. Good and evil came into the world; an old story. The sudden breakdown of isolation and prejudice did not last, though it did not entirely go away either. The 'God virus', as some called it became a blessing as well as a disease.

The irony is that those who started it remained secret. Like Marconi, they transmitted something world-changing from a remote location, but without his transmitting and receiving equipment. I had got the message to return to this secret place, where we had invented a real revelation for the world, which we now had to hide from. I was sick of reading minds myself, especially in the Onego snacking aisle. I could feel the wondrous unity underneath but I did not want to know the rest. The fears, lusts and madness of puerile humanity, just like mine, just like children. Luckily I knew, without any aid, how to block everything. Maybe I needed someone with a bladder, but I knew I was leaving, to go to the happy isles where this hope had been released into the world. Can Adam and Eve go back to Eden for a meeting about the future? I doubted it but I had to go to that remotest of places, where all things were hidden, all things revealed.

The story is about the balance of the private, inward-looking world of the individual being exploited, versus the public world of outside possibility of the future, where all is changed, all is connected, all is magic. Prophecy depends on the public world. Disappearing into the private world – not caring what effects your words have – means no sense of future and is therefore a narrowing of mind, giving only an appearance of width. Literature depends, like magic, on real connections, on a wider sense of the public world and there will be a move back to a truly wider world, an off-grid true reconnection.

Write About

If the future is a combination of science and magic, ask yourself how you see your future, personally and in terms of the world and, using a combination of knowledge and intuition, describe it.

Use the three-part structure of the prophetic poems above (vantage point, present and past, then prophecy) to create a vision of the future.

Parody a bucket list or five-year plan with the real story of future events.

Write about a baffled prophet who closes his business 'due to unforeseen circumstances'.

Investigators of mechanical consciousness find God.

Write a modern take of 'The Machine Stops'.

The Voynich Manuscript has never been translated. Research it and imagine what it says about the future.

The millennial breakdown of 1999 (as predicted by Nostradamus) did not happen – or did it?

Write an obscure prophecy in verse, then write an interpretation of it.

Magical Texts and Literary Examples

Magical

Joseph Campbell. 'The Occult in Myth and History' (1977), from *The Mythic Dimension* (1997).
Jeffrey J. Kripal. *Authors of the Impossible* (2010).
Gary Lachman. *A Secret History of Consciousness* (2003).
Nostradamus. (1555; available online).

Literary Examples

Matthew Arnold. 'Dover Beach' (1867).
Leonard Cohen. *The Future* (1992).
E.M. Forster. 'The Machine Stops' (1909).
Michel Houellebecq. *Submission* (2015).
Christopher Priest. *The Glamour* (1984).
W.B. Yeats. 'The Second Coming' (1919).

Index